S. Hrg. 111–1047

A STRONGER WORKFORCE INVESTMENT SYSTEM FOR A STRONGER ECONOMY

I0454866

HEARING

OF THE

COMMITTEE ON HEALTH, EDUCATION, LABOR, AND PENSIONS

UNITED STATES SENATE

ONE HUNDRED ELEVENTH CONGRESS

SECOND SESSION

ON

EXAMINING A STRONGER WORKFORCE INVESTMENT SYSTEM FOR A STRONGER ECONOMY

FEBRUARY 24, 2010

Printed for the use of the Committee on Health, Education, Labor, and Pensions

Available via the World Wide Web: http://www.gpo.gov/fdsys/

U.S. GOVERNMENT PRINTING OFFICE

55–207 PDF   WASHINGTON : 2011

For sale by the Superintendent of Documents, U.S. Government Printing Office
Internet: bookstore.gpo.gov   Phone: toll free (866) 512–1800; DC area (202) 512–1800
Fax: (202) 512–2104   Mail: Stop IDCC, Washington, DC 20402–0001

COMMITTEE ON HEALTH, EDUCATION, LABOR, AND PENSIONS

TOM HARKIN, Iowa, *Chairman*

CHRISTOPHER J. DODD, Connecticut
BARBARA A. MIKULSKI, Maryland
JEFF BINGAMAN, New Mexico
PATTY MURRAY, Washington
JACK REED, Rhode Island
BERNARD SANDERS (I), Vermont
SHERROD BROWN, Ohio
ROBERT P. CASEY, JR., Pennsylvania
KAY R. HAGAN, North Carolina
JEFF MERKLEY, Oregon
AL FRANKEN, Minnesota
MICHAEL F. BENNET, Colorado

MICHAEL B. ENZI, Wyoming
JUDD GREGG, New Hampshire
LAMAR ALEXANDER, Tennessee
RICHARD BURR, North Carolina
JOHNNY ISAKSON, Georgia
JOHN McCAIN, Arizona
ORRIN G. HATCH, Utah
LISA MURKOWSKI, Alaska
TOM COBURN, M.D., Oklahoma
PAT ROBERTS, Kansas

DANIEL SMITH, *Staff Director*
FRANK MACCHIAROLA, *Republican Staff Director and Chief Counsel*

(II)

CONTENTS

STATEMENTS

WEDNESDAY, FEBRUARY 24, 2010

(III)

VerDate Nov 24 2008   15:12 Aug 22, 2011   Jkt 035165   PO 00000   Frm 00004   Fmt 5904   Sfmt 5904   S:\DOCS\55207.TXT   DENISE

A STRONGER WORKFORCE INVESTMENT SYSTEM FOR A STRONGER ECONOMY

WEDNESDAY, FEBRUARY 24, 2010

U.S. SENATE,
COMMITTEE ON HEALTH, EDUCATION, LABOR, AND PENSIONS,
Washington, DC.

The committee met, pursuant to notice, at 11:00 a.m. in Room SD–430, Dirksen Senate Office Building, Hon. Tom Harkin, chairman of the committee, presiding.

Present: Senators Harkin, Reed, Brown, Casey, Franken, and Enzi.

OPENING STATEMENT OF SENATOR HARKIN

The CHAIRMAN. The Health, Education, Labor, and Pensions Committee will come to order.

Today, we are starting a series of hearings on the reauthorization of the Workforce Investment Act, which, by the way, has not been reauthorized since 2003, and there have been a lot of changes in our country, in the workforce, and in what we need for future economic success in this country since that point in time.

I apologize. We have two votes, as you know, and I assume that others will be showing up here in due course. I apologize at the beginning. I have a healthcare meeting that I have to attend at 11 a.m., and the Senator from Pennsylvania, Senator Casey, has graciously volunteered to take over the chair when I have to leave, and I appreciate that very much.

Senator Enzi, I assume, will be here very shortly.

In his State of the Union address last month, President Obama made clear his commitment to getting Americans back to work. As he put it, job creation is "our No. 1 focus for 2010."

That is why we must act swiftly to ensure that American workers have the education, skills training, and supports they need to compete and thrive in a 21st century global job market, and that is why we have convened this hearing today to examine the future of the Workforce Investment Act, as we move toward reauthorization of this important program.

I want to thank all of my colleagues on this committee, especially our Ranking Member, Senator Enzi, and also Senators Murray and Isakson, who, as chair and Ranking Member of the Employment and Workplace Safety Subcommittee, have shown great leadership over the past decade on issues relating to workforce development. I appreciate their work and their partnership on reauthorizing WIA, as we call it, the Workforce Investment Act.

(1)

I also want to thank their staffs, who continue to work tirelessly and in a bipartisan fashion.

And I thank our witnesses for being here today.

Despite some success of the Recovery Act in jump-starting some economic growth, the official national unemployment rate remains high at just under 10 percent. In my State, it is about 7 percent.

In part, these harsh realities are the consequences of an unusually deep recession, but they also reflect a lack of training and education in large segments of our workforce. Recent studies indicate that more than 40 percent of U.S. workers do not have the basic skills to do their jobs. In an era of massive layoffs and downsizing, it is more important than ever that job seekers have access to the education and training they need to shift careers and adjust to a changing economy.

Developing and maintaining a highly trained and highly educated workforce is paramount for our economic success. If businesses are unable to find workers in this country who have the education and training to fill the jobs of the 21st century, they will be compelled to look abroad to remain competitive, and our economy will suffer accordingly.

Today, we will hear from experts who are working to improve and strengthen our Nation's workforce development system. I read most of the summaries of your testimonies, last evening. They are very good. I appreciate that.

All of your full statements will be made a part of the record in their entirety, and I would hope that each of you would summarize them so that we can get into a discussion with you on that.

I look forward to hearing about ways to encourage collaboration, shared accountability for the education and employment needs of all Americans, especially to those with barriers to employment. I am especially interested in what we do to help people with disabilities get into the workplace.

I mentioned that we have about 10 percent unemployment in this country. Now, it is higher among African-Americans, higher among Hispanics, teens. That pales in comparison with the unemployment statistics among people with disabilities. About 64 percent of people with disabilities who want to work, who are capable of working, are unemployed—64 percent. That ought to shock our conscience.

These are people who want to work—can work with a modicum of support, with the help of the ADA and other things that we have done—who can be employed. We need to find how we can train them and get them equipped again to enter and advance in the job market of the 21st century.

Again, I thank our expert witnesses for being here. I will introduce each of you as we go along. I will leave the record open at this point for Senator Enzi to make his opening statement when he arrives, if he would care to do so.

First, we have Anthony P. Carnevale, a research professor and director of the Georgetown University Center on Education and the Workforce. Mr. Carnevale will discuss the importance of the workforce investment system in supporting the education and employment needs of job seekers, workers, and employers.

Joseph M. Carbone—it is Carbone?

Mr. CARBONE. Yes.

The CHAIRMAN. President and chief executive officer of The WorkPlace, Inc., of Connecticut. Mr. Carbone will describe his work to integrate workforce investment services for individuals with disabilities.

Mr. Paul Stalknecht, president and CEO of Air Conditioning Contractors of America. Mr. Stalknecht is a business leader who will describe his engagement with the workforce system as a business owner.

Then we have Cheryl Feldman, executive director, District 1199C Training and Upgrading Fund at the Breslin Learning Center in Pennsylvania. Ms. Feldman will describe the role that labor can play in partnership with business to develop education and employment programs that lead to good jobs.

And we have Robert Templin, president of the Northern Virginia Community College, NOVA. Mr. Templin will discuss the value of sector partnerships, those that align education and employment training services to the employment needs of a particular industry or employer, and the role that education should play in supporting the workforce investment system.

I might just add, Mr. Templin, I met with some people from the Iowa community colleges earlier this morning, and they were talking about this bill and how community colleges can be integrated into this whole system. I look forward to hearing more about that, about how community colleges can be involved.

With that, I will recognize Mr. Carnevale, who, of course, is no stranger to this committee and has been involved in job training and workforce development issues for a number of years.

Again, your testimony will be made part of the record. If you summarize it—we will leave it at 5 minutes. If you need a little more than that, don't worry about it.

STATEMENT OF ANTHONY P. CARNEVALE, RESEARCH PRO-FESSOR AND DIRECTOR, GEORGETOWN UNIVERSITY CEN-TER ON EDUCATION AND THE WORKFORCE, WASHINGTON, DC

Mr. CARNEVALE. One point I want to make early on is that I think, and I think most people agree, we are in the early phases of a recovery. I think, when all is said and done, the National Bureau of Economic Research will say that the recession officially ended in November or December of this past year.

That doesn't mean that we are going to have a robust jobs recovery. I think we all agree, who fool with these things, that we are not talking about unemployment anywhere below 9.2 or 9.3 this year and that we have a slow, long, and what is often called a jobless recovery. That is, the economy will recover a long time before it starts creating the jobs we need.

It is the case, I think pretty clearly, that over the next decade or so, given the size of the baby boom retirement especially, that we will create something on the order of 47 million jobs, with about 14 million new jobs. The rest will be jobs that we get because people retire.

The striking thing about those jobs is that a very substantial share, about 64 percent, will require some kind of post-secondary education or training. Not necessarily a college degree, maybe a certificate or an industry-based certification or also a B.A., and so on. The essential change in the American labor market, especially since 1980, has been the increasing demand for post-secondary level skill of various kinds.

In a sense, we are not set up to deal with this. We have a Labor Department that deals with jobs, an Education Department that deals with education, and we don't connect the two very well. My bias is that the Obama budget provides us an opportunity to begin doing that.

The President has requested $261 million set aside for innovations that would link or, as his budget statement says, break down the silos between the Education Department and Labor Department. And I really do believe that in terms of helping Americans quickly and effectively and not to mention cost effectively, that linking education and education programs and training programs with real jobs is the way that we are going to have to start thinking about doing this, especially given the fiscal austerity we face going forward.

I would argue for a couple of things. One is where we can get it, and it is always scarce. We need to try and get learning and earning programs, where employers and education and training institutions, public and private, participate together to provide learning that includes learning in a classroom and learning on the job. Those are always hard to come by.

The easier thing to do is to build compressed learning programs. Instead of taking 2 years to get an A.A., programs that march straight through and do it in 12 or 13 months max. Or a certificate in 7 or 8 months, where you go to school pretty much full-time if you can. If not, you go every Saturday for 8 to 10 months with a lot of the frills and extra education along the way cut out.

It is the only way that experienced workers and people who are working, which is the vast majority of college students now as well, can really move through these systems with any speed and effectiveness. And finally, I think none of this will work very well until we build information systems and counseling that tell people where the jobs are, how much they will make, that will make some sense of the education they get as they try to move toward employment.

A couple final points. One is that we have moved tens of millions of people through UI. That is the people who have applied for unemployment insurance since the recession began. Very few of them ever got talked to or got counseling or ran into an information system that helped them figure out what their prospects were. They were left untouched and feel untouched, I think.

The second thing is that the information systems to do this are available. We just had some difficulty because of the silos in our governmental systems in hooking these things to education and training programs.

Thank you, Mr. Chairman.

[The prepared statement of Dr. Carnevale follows:]

PREPARED STATEMENT OF ANTHONY P. CARNEVALE

The mismatch between job growth and skill is a growing problem in the American economy. Thus, our ability to align our huge investments in post-secondary education and training programs funded by DOE with job openings and labor market services funded by DOL has become crucial. This mismatch will only accelerate over the next 3 years as the economy recovers and moves back toward a 5 percent non-inflationary rate of unemployment. The Obama administration has given us a strong start in aligning DOL and DOE programs by asking for a set aside of $261 million "breaking down program silos" between DOE and DOL by creating "Workforce Innovation Partnerships."

Our own projections at The Georgetown Center on Education and the Workforce (The Center) show a painfully slow but robust recovery. We aren't likely to recover our pre-recession job levels for another 24 months. And it will be 36 more months before we achieve an unemployment rate approaching 5 percent and create enough jobs to employ the new job seekers who came into the labor market since December 2007 when this recession began.

We are back from the brink of economic collapse and I strongly suspect that National Bureau of Economic Research will eventually decide—retrospectively—that this recession ended sometime between November of last year and March of this year. 2010 should end with net positive job growth. The recession may be over in this technical sense but it is far from over in labor markets. Our own projections at The Center find that we won't recover the 8 million-plus jobs we've lost until 2012. It may take us until 2015 to get back to the jobs we lost and add enough new jobs to employ the newly minted entrants job seekers who have come into the workforce since the recession began.

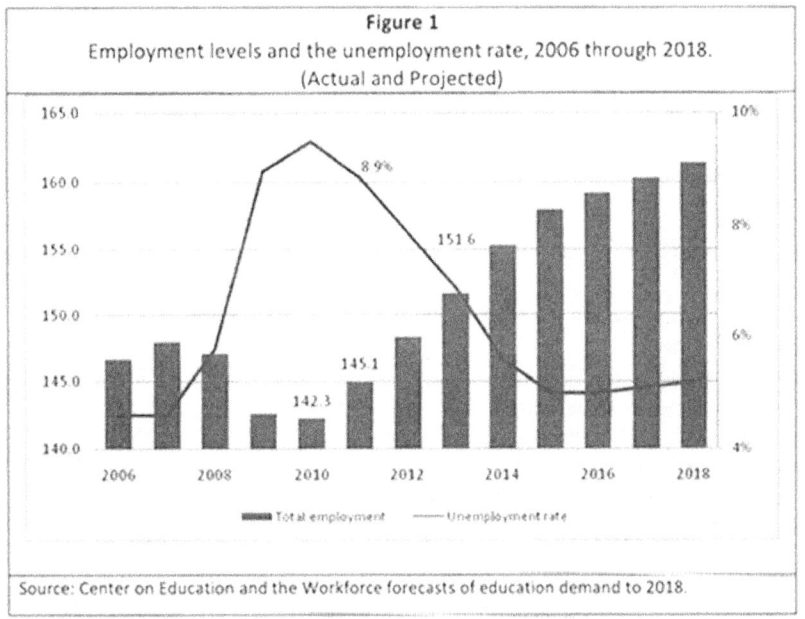

Figure 1

Employment levels and the unemployment rate, 2006 through 2018.
(Actual and Projected)

Source: Center on Education and the Workforce forecasts of education demand to 2018.

Jobs that require at least some post-secondary education will lead the recovery. The future of job growth in the United States is one in which more and more workers will require post-secondary education or training. Between 2008 and 2018, the economy will create 47 million job openings—consisting of 14 million net new jobs and 33 million replacement jobs, those necessary to replace workers who retire, become disabled or die (see Figure 2). ***Nearly two-thirds of these jobs—about 64 percent—will require workers who have at least some college education or better.*** Some 34 percent will require at least a Bachelor's degree, while 30 percent will require some college or a 2-year Associate's degree. Only 36 percent of those 47 million jobs will require workers with only a high school diploma or less.

As the recovery proceeds slowly over the next 3 years there will be a growing mismatch between job openings and growing post-secondary education and training requirements. Our success in helping our fellow Americans in adapting to these new labor market realities will depend more and more on our ability to break down the silos between our post-secondary education and training programs, job openings and career pathways.

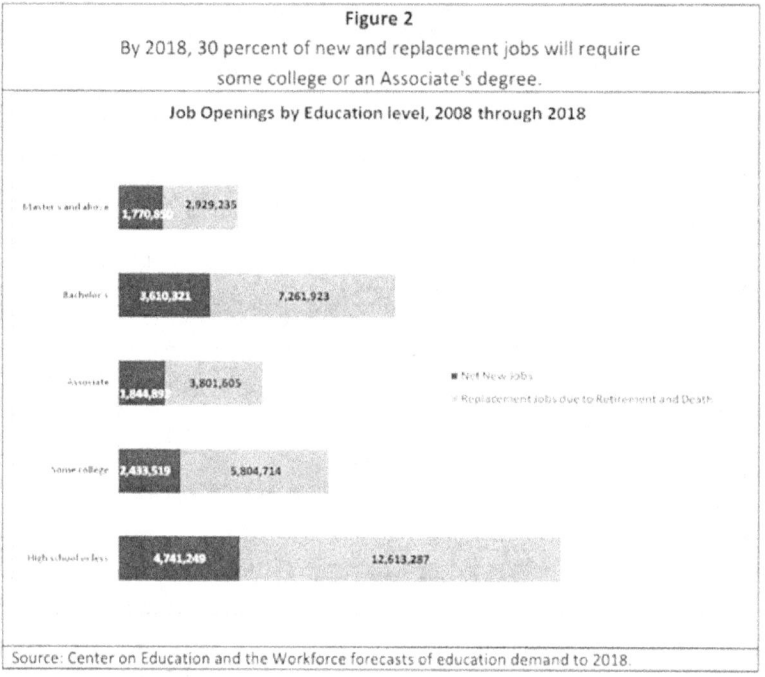

Figure 2

By 2018, 30 percent of new and replacement jobs will require some college or an Associate's degree.

Job Openings by Education level, 2008 through 2018

Source: Center on Education and the Workforce forecasts of education demand to 2018.

If we fail, many existing and new workers will be left behind as the wage structure continues to take the shape of an hour-glass with the post-secondary educated and trained workers concentrating at the top and the workers with high school or less falling towards the bottom.

Our projections show that between now and 2018 the economy will create 30 million jobs that will require at least some college or better but if current trends continue:

• We will fall short of meeting the demand by at least 3 million college-educated Americans.

• A growing share of Americans will be left behind with no access to the middle class as industry and occupational growth as well as wage advantages shifts away from jobs that require only high school or less and towards industries and occupations that require at least some post-secondary education or training.

• If the past is any guide this shortfall will raise the wages of post-secondary haves vs. post-secondary have-nots as the recovery picks up momentum.

Technology is automating repetitive tasks and activities in jobs. As a result, more and more jobs tasks and activities left to people at work are non-repetitive. Sometimes these tasks and activities require high school or less, like working at a fast food outlet or digging a ditch. Other times, in professional, managerial and technical jobs, these non-repetitive tasks require high levels of knowledge, skills and developed abilities.

The non-repetitive tasks in professional, managerial and technical jobs tend to require post-secondary levels of knowledge, skills and developed abilities. These educated workers have been in increasing demand since the mid-1980s so their wages are much higher than people who perform non-repetitive tasks in low-wage jobs. As a result, the wages of post-secondary educated workers have been rising relative to workers with high school or less (the rise faltering briefly in 2001–2002 and of course during the recessions) ever since the mid-1980s.

The industries with the highest concentrations of post-secondary educated workers are growing the fastest leaving workers with high school or less stranded in sometimes large, but slow growing low-wage industries. For many workers these low-wage jobs should be transitional but are not because of education barriers to mobility.

The top tier of employers with post-secondary concentrations includes a cluster of fast-growing services industries. These each have workforces dominated—75 percent to 90 percent—by workers with at least some post-secondary education or training. These include:

- Information Services;
- Professional and Business Services;
- Financial Services;
- Private Education and Training Services;
- Healthcare Services; and
- Government and Public Education Services.

The middle tier of post-secondary concentration includes Construction and a set of old line services industries where the share of workers with higher education hovers around 50 percent. These include:

- Construction;
- Transportation and Utilities Services;
- Wholesale and Retail Trade Services;
- Leisure and Hospitality Services; and
- Personal Services.

The bottom tier includes mostly goods production in Manufacturing and Natural Resources, where the share of post-secondary workers ranges between 30 percent and 40 percent of industry workforces.

Demand for post-secondary education is tied more closely to occupations than industries. With the exception of healthcare support occupations, occupations with the fastest growth have the highest share of post-secondary education.

Occupational clusters with the most intensive concentrations of post-secondary workers include:

- Science, Technology, Engineering, Mathematics and Social Science (STEM), 93 percent;
- Education and Training Occupations, 93 percent;
- Healthcare Practitioners and Technicians, 92 percent;
- Community Services, 89 percent; and
- Managerial and Professional Office occupations, 83 percent.

Those five clusters represent more than 20 percent of total occupational employment and 45 percent of all jobs for post-secondary workers.

A second tier of post-secondary intensity includes two occupational clusters where more than half of the incumbent workers have at least some college education or better. These are:

- Sales and Office Support, 60 percent; and
- Healthcare Support occupations, 52 percent.

A third tier of occupations consists of two clusters where less than half of the workers have at least some college education or better, including:

- Food and Personal Services, 41 percent; and
- Blue Collar occupations, 34 percent.

WIA and the Employment Services still provide irreplaceable income support and labor market services that connect education and training to real jobs, but the core human capital development function in workforce development has shifted to DOE [1] (1) making access to post-secondary education and training a crucial programmatic element in employment policy and (2) making employability a crucial performance standard for secondary and post-secondary education.

My own view is that the committee should focus on breaking down the silos between the U.S. Employment Services, the One-Stops and the Nations' education, training and retraining providers, especially in secondary and post-secondary education and training. Breaking down the silos between our Department of Labor

---

[1] This shift has been reflected in appropriations in the case in the United States since the 1980–1981 recession. In the 1980–1981 recession, the intuitive programmatic response to the jobs problem heavily favored employment and short term training policy over education policy. The programmatic centerpiece that grew out of the Carter stimulus in response to the 1980–1981 recession was the Comprehensive Employment and Training Act (CETA). The core programmatic mission in response to the jobs problem was led by the Employment and Training Administration (ETA) in the U.S. Department of Labor. "Employment and training policy" peaked in the Carter years.

CETA and its progeny, The Job Training Partnership Act (JTPA) and the current Workforce Investment Act (WIA) have waned ever since 1979. If WIA, the current version of CETA, were to be funded at the same levels in the last Carter budget, it would be funded at almost $25 billion. WIA the current version of CETA is funded somewhere between $3 and $4 billion.

(DOL) and Department of Education (DOE) programs is crucial to both successful workforce development and successful secondary and post-secondary education policies.

Both the Labor and Education Departments have a role in building a modern workforce development system. The Employment and Training Administration (ETA) of the U.S. Department of Labor provides critical employment services and a real world connection to real jobs in real labor markets. Post-Secondary education, especially community colleges, have become the crucial education and training provider for workforce development and retraining. Making the connection between the WIA on one side of the mall and post-secondary education on the other is the crucial element in the development of an effective workforce development and retraining system.

The Obama administration has given us a place to start. In its DOL budget request for fiscal year 2011 the Administration is asking for a setaside of $261 million to create Workforce Innovation Partnership between DOE and DOL for "breaking down program silos" including a 5 percent setaside for "learn and earn programs."

President Obama's new budget proposal is the first on record that explicitly recognizes the need to integrate WIA and USDOE programs. It's Department of Labor Budget request proposes:

" (A) Workforce Innovation Partnership with the Department of Education and establishes two innovation funds that will support and test promising approaches to job training as well as encourage States and localities to work across programmatic silos to improve services."

We can best use the $261 million requested in President Obama's 2011 Budget for "breaking down program silos" between DOL and DOE for funding demonstration projects that develop existing best practices such as:

• Highly structured *"learn and earn programs"* like apprenticeship and on-the-job training," as requested by the President;

• *Compressed occupational training programs* that integrate basic skills preparation with fast and intensive occupational training leading to post-secondary certificates with previously demonstrated labor market value;

• *Job and skill counseling* for unemployed and underemployed experienced workers and working students tied to state-of-the-art information on earnings trajectories and career pathways;

• *Accountability systems for maximizing the labor market value of post-secondary education and training programs* by tying post-secondary transcript data funded under the ARRA with employer wage records data currently housed in the U.S. Employment Services.

And for statewide and nationwide development of on-line job search systems (*Job Exchanges*) tied to (*Learning Exchanges*) that match job openings and career pathways to available courses offered by post-secondary institutions as well as on-line courseware.

The CHAIRMAN. Thank you, Mr. Carnevale. I will follow up later about the role of community colleges, too, in that education.

I yield now to our Ranking Member, Senator Enzi, who has been a great leader in this area for many, many years.

OPENING STATEMENT OF SENATOR ENZI

Senator ENZI. Thank you, Mr. Chairman.

I apologize for being late. I want to thank you for holding the hearing on this important issue.

The Senate has done a good job on this twice before. We passed it unanimously through the Senate. I am glad that we are working off of that bill and working to get something done. I suspect, and from what I have read in the statements, that we are probably in agreement with everybody.

I appreciate your comments about the community college because they are an important part of education and workforce development to the recovery of our economy. This hearing is also important because we are really talking about jobs. While we need to create more jobs, that isn't enough. We need to create a workforce that has the skills to fill those jobs.

The facts are that 8 in 10 jobs require some skilled post-secondary credential. Yet more than 12 million adults in the labor force today don't have a high school credential. More than 18 million adults between the ages of 18 and 64 have not graduated from high school and, therefore, do not qualify for most of the jobs in the current economy. Over 51 million adults in the same age range have no college education and are in low-wage jobs.

Additionally, occupations that usually require a post-secondary degree are expected to account for nearly half of all new jobs from 2008 to 2018 and a third of all total job openings. Workers without skills won't be able to take advantage of new job opportunities. Any gains in employment will be short-lived, and employers will be unable to find the skilled workforce they need to grow and compete.

The jobs that will be created when our economy picks up will be middle skill jobs that require education and training beyond the high school level. Workers have to be ready to fill these jobs by quickly acquiring new skills and having ongoing access to quality education and skills training so they can turn those jobs into careers.

According to a recent Business Roundtable report, 60 percent of businesses are experiencing difficulty in finding qualified applicants for *current* job openings. This is occurring despite our high unemployment rates. Business depends on having workers with the necessary skills to perform jobs safely and effectively.

Our economy depends on business to expand and create jobs—which cannot happen if skilled workers are not available to fill those jobs. What we are discussing today is a way to help solve this problem and not only put people back to work, but help them keep their jobs and advance in their jobs.

It has been over 10 years since WIA was first enacted, and now, more than ever, we need to modernize and strengthen the system, building on what has worked. America's workers and employers need to be confident that the workforce development system will provide the skills that are needed to keep jobs in America and keep us competitive in the 21st century economy.

With an unemployment rate of almost 10 percent and a widening skills gap for our students and workers, we need to have in place a workforce development system that will meet the challenges of the global economy and the 21st century workplace. We need to help workers secure the skills they need for the jobs being created as our economy comes out of the economic downturn, and we need to make sure that employers have skilled workers in order to be competitive.

I am pleased that we will hear today from a panel of witnesses who understand what a successful workforce development system is. A strong education and workforce development system is critical for our students and workers to be prepared to meet the ever-escalating knowledge and skills of the 21st century.

For this reason, I am committed to working with the Administration and my Senate and House colleagues to put together a bipartisan bill that reauthorizes, strengthens, and modernizes WIA, a complete jobs bill. I would mention again that it has been the

House that we have had trouble getting this through, but I have mentioned to Chairman Miller every time that I see him that we need to get WIA done, and he is in agreement. But we will have to get that last step done.

Thank you, Mr. Chairman.

The CHAIRMAN. Well, thank you very much, Senator Enzi. Hopefully, we can get it done. We have got to get it done this year. We have just got to. We are going to get it done.

Again, I apologize. I have to leave to go to a healthcare meeting. Senator Casey has agreed to——

Senator ENZI. I understand. We are all working on the healthcare problem.

[Laughter.]

We can get something done.

The CHAIRMAN. Thank you.

STATEMENT OF SENATOR CASEY

Senator CASEY [presiding]. Well, thank you very much.

Why don't we continue with the witnesses' statements?

Mr. Carbone.

STATEMENT OF JOSEPH M. CARBONE, PRESIDENT AND CEO, THE WORKPLACE, INC., SOUTHWESTERN CONNECTICUT'S WORKFORCE DEVELOPMENT BOARD, BRIDGEPORT, CT

Mr. CARBONE. OK. Thank you very, very much, Senator, and thank you for inviting me.

I am Joe Carbone. I am president and CEO for The Workplace, Inc. We act as the WIB for southwestern Connecticut.

In some respects, Congress has been looking at the reauthorization issue for a good number of years, and I think that it has worked to our advantage because we now have a chance to evaluate our system from the perspective of how it has operated during times of real good economy and exactly how it would operate in a very, very bad economy, the recession.

I think that the experience—and I speak for my region, and I have been there for 14 years—is such that I can feel that the system is certainly fundamentally sound, but it is not perfect. There are certain elements to this system that I think are worth preserving and, I think, have enabled the American workforce system, under the Workforce Investment Act, to play a critical role in advancing careers for people and meeting the needs for businesses.

Part of the act was to create this hub in the system that we call the One-Stop, and I think experience in the last 10, 11, 12 years is such that the One-Stops are natural kinds of magnets for people who need our assistance and businesses who need our help as well. Workforce investment boards can be a neutral broker. When you put together a collaboration of many different kinds of partners, some of which actually compete with one another, it is important to have an agent of fairness at the very top of that system. I think that has worked well.

They are business-led. A majority of the members of the board are from business, and in many cases, they serve not just as members of the board, but to help to kind of alert boards to trends and things that are happening with respect to businesses' needs that are very, very important.

The partner base of any One-Stop system, as I mentioned before, is extremely diverse, and you do not just have the required partners in your system, but you—by the very nature of the region, you can add partners that might be from the faith-based area. Organized labor play a major role in programs in my region.

It is important that the workforce board, workforce investment board use part of this act as sort of the glue for the system, keeping everybody together and keeping everyone's time and efforts as really productive as possible.

Clearly, the system is showing that it is flexible. It can respond in times of prosperity, and it can easily make the shift if we have a period of a recession like we just experienced.

The way the act was written, it brings the free-market system into our business. I think that was a very, very important feature. With respect to contracts that are offered by workforce investment boards, they are all out there, and they are bid in a competitive way. The training community, where people get ITAs, individual training accounts, you have choice for customer, and you have a system that workforce boards can make richer and richer every day, taking, again, the for-profit trainers, the not-for-profit, and the public.

Now, all of this happens as workforce investments boards under this system get money that is the so-called "formula dollars." That opens the doors and creates the system on a local level. Communities have choice. If communities wish to simply administer the three lines of funding, they can do that. If they wish to make workforce development an enterprise of sort, they can do that.

With respect to the integration of services, there is value added created every time that that happens. It is a very important feature for all boards to pursue.

A couple of ideas with respect to disability services, and I know this is important to Senator Harkin. We took the Office of Vocational Rehabilitation Services, which is part of the State, the Bureau for the Blind, and we actually created a situation where the conferencing of cases are done with caseworkers in our One-Stop system. So nothing is lost. Nothing is missed. They can take advantage of every possible program that is out there that can be helpful.

We have done the same with respect to youth programs, using business to create interns, using foundations to help us create Web sites and other mechanisms that can help to advance the interest of young people. We have done the same with respect to veterans, involving institutions that offer them residential places to stay, services of our State Department of Labor and other entities that can work with the partnership at the One-Stop level.

I have seven ideas of ways in which I think this committee and the reauthorization process can make the workforce investment boards at the ground level better. If they are better at the ground level, it is better services to everybody.

Provide incentives for WIBs to think and operate in a regional way.

Provide incentives for WIBs to leverage the formula dollars to grow the business. Formula dollars alone do not allow imagination or innovation in the system. It is important that they think "grow the business" all the time.

Provide incentives for WIBs to create real value added through the integration of services and partners. Most times, that doesn't happen, and it doesn't simply happen because it is mentioned in the act. The WIBs must earn the respect of everybody to make it happen.

Provide incentives to States to explore a data-driven system to determine workforce investment districts, the catchment districts. There is a science to good districts that contribute to an exciting workforce system, and it is important that that happened.

There ought to be incentives provided so that States and local areas increase the number of ITAs, that is the fruit of our labor, one of the most important things that we do every single year.

I was asked to give a couple of examples of where this kind of "grow the business" mentality has helped us in our region. This approach in my region, southwestern Connecticut, 36 percent of my budget is formula dollars, and 64 percent is nonformula dollars. You can do this best if you are a 501(c)(3) and not part of Government, but it means that you can actively compete for Federal, State, and other competitive grants. You can solicit contributions that are basically philanthropic in nature from foundations.

With respect to competitive grants—and we have won many in disability services, in veterans services, in the green sector, and many others—they total about $50 million in the last several years for us. With respect to ITAs, we have raised over $4 million from the private sector, and that has enabled us to grant 1,700 more people opportunities to get trained.

I can go on, but let me just make one last point. There are two creative things that I think are important to this committee. With respect to our summer programs, we had over 700 youth employed. We made a conscious choice to dedicate a quarter of the jobs to kids with certifiable disabilities.

We had 25 percent of them. They worked for businesses. We had contracts with 80 for-profit businesses. They had meaningful experiences throughout the summer. A good workforce board will have the contacts with businesses to make that happen.

In addition to that, we created a mortgage crisis job training program, which links the job training system with the foreclosure problems in our State. We are doing it for the whole State of Connecticut. We are at the table when families are facing foreclosure and need to grow earnings. There is a chart in the information that I filed that shows the value of education with respect to growing wages.

All of that is very important. That has been our experience. I think it is a choice between whether you are simply administering the programs of the Workforce Investment Act or whether you grow your business and make it an exciting place to be.

Thank you very much.

[The prepared statement of Mr. Carbone follows:]

THE WORKPLACE, INC.,
BRIDGEPORT, CT 06604,
February 24, 2010.

Senator TOM HARKIN, *Chairman,*
Committee on Health, Education, Labor, and Pensions,
U.S. Senate,
Washington, DC 20510–6300.

Re: Testimony for "A Stronger Workforce Investment System for a Stronger Economy" Hearing

DEAR SENATOR HARKIN AND HELP COMMITTEE MEMBERS: Thank you for the opportunity to provide input on this important topic. The American workforce system has the potential to play a pivotal role in economic recovery and regional competitiveness, as I hope my testimony will illustrate.

My organization, The WorkPlace, Inc., is a private 501(c)(3) not-for-profit which has served as southwestern Connecticut's Workforce Investment Board (and predecessor Private Industry Council) for 26 years. Although there are some differences in how States set up their systems, and differences in local market needs and priorities, our experience is broadly representative. Like other WIB's, we are guided by a Board of Directors representing business, labor, and other WIA-mandated partners and key stakeholders.

Thank you very much for the opportunity to share these thoughts with you.

JOSEPH M. CARBONE,
President and Chief Executive Officer, The WorkPlace, Inc.

––––––

PREPARED STATEMENT OF JOSEPH M. CARBONE

"MOVING BEYOND THE FORMULA"

1. THE CRITICAL ROLE THE WORKFORCE INVESTMENT SYSTEM PLAYS IN ADDRESSING THE EMPLOYMENT, EDUCATION, AND SKILL NEEDS OF ITS DUAL CUSTOMERS—WORKERS, JOB SEEKERS AND EMPLOYERS

The system is fundamentally sound but imperfect.

• It has **responded** to the challenge of a recession far beyond what was imagined by the makers of the Workforce Investment Act (WIA).

• The Act enables WIBs to play a critical role during times of recession as well as prosperity.

- **One-Stops are the hub** of the system; they act as natural magnets for unemployed, underemployed, and employed individuals, as well as businesses needing workers.
- Workforce Investment Boards (WIB's) can be **neutral brokers**, which is a necessary factor in bringing together many diverse and competing partners.
- WIBs are **business-led**, and they become the natural place for businesses to turn to when they need workers.
- WIBs connect **partners**; the Act identifies the required partners and suggests others as well. However, it takes WIBs with credibility to keep the partnership together and make it productive.
- WIBs are **flexible** and able to change as economic conditions dictate; for example less training and more education in a deep & prolonged downturn.
- The Workforce Investment Act enables WIBs to lead a **free-market** system of job training. As a regional planning entity and not a competitor for training business, they can select from proposals and programs from for-profit, not-for-profit, and government providers. The customer and taxpayer interest can come first.
- **Formula funding** provides the seeds for the local system, as well as program support.
- WIB's received **ARRA**/stimulus investments under similar rules to the formula funds, which enabled the system to adjust to the new requirements brought about by high unemployment and many new customers needing service.
- The Workforce Investment Act offers **local communities a choice**—their WIB can be the administrator of the three pools of funding under the formula system, or they can choose to do that PLUS a far more enterprising approach.

2. NEW AND INNOVATIVE PRACTICES USED TO BETTER INTEGRATE SERVICES TO MORE EFFECTIVELY MEET THE NEEDS OF WORKERS AND EMPLOYERS, INCLUDING BARRIERS TO SUCH PRACTICES

Some WIBs and One-Stops are finding creative ways to work with multiple partners to better integrate services. Here are a few examples from our experience in Connecticut:

- **Older Workers** have been fully integrated into the One-Stop system. By using SCSEP (Senior Community Service Employment Program) as a true training model, we have been able to provide skills upgrades and job placements to unemployed workers over age 55. We leverage and integrate the following:
  - WIA Core Services (job search, computer workshops, professional development)
  - Community Colleges (skills training certificates)
  - Local Government (serve as host agencies)
  - Business (Adecco and other placement agencies have signed on to place older workers in skill-specific permanent placements. GoliathJobs.com has developed a Web site specifically to connect older workers with job openings.)

- **People With Disabilities:** The Voc-Rehab agencies (e.g. Bureau of Rehabilitative Services and Bureau of Education Services for the Blind) are on-site in our Bridgeport One-Stop once per week to do **case conferencing** with One-Stop staff. In addition, we utilize our PWI (Projects With Industry grant) funding to provide placement, working closely with local employers.

- **Youth:** targeted youth programs have helped to provide more services to at-risk youth. With private funding (JPMorgan Chase and others) we have established the following:
  - **A youth Web site**, designed by Bridgeport students, whose content includes job training, employment, and college resources.
  - An **allied health exploration** program that provides students the opportunity to understand careers in allied health (beyond nursing assistant) and to work as interns during the summer.
  - **Summer internships** in the arts, and with local industrial employers (including Sikorsky and Derecktor Shipyards).
  - In each of these programs, we work with the local school system and the business partner to identify the appropriate kids. This could not have happened with WIA dollars due to the stringent income guidelines and the performance outcomes.

- **Veterans:** our program for Homeless Veterans built partnerships with Homes for the Brave (a residential center for homeless veterans), the VA Hospital, Department of Labor Veterans Services, and many other local agencies. Veterans in the program received intensive career services, training, job placement, and permanent housing through a multi-level collaboration.

- **Community Resource Center:** in response to the deep and prolonged recession, we got funding from the local United Way to use our One-Stop as a point of delivery for meeting basic needs. This new Center awarded small grants for rental assistance, utilities, and transportation. In addition, the Center partnered with local agencies that provided assistance to people in need of food, shelter, housing, day care, medical insurance, and legal services. This created a stronger network of partners and expanded awareness of services available in the One-Stop.

3. WAYS TO PROMOTE INNOVATION IN THE STRUCTURE AND DELIVERY OF AMERICA'S WORKFORCE SYSTEM TO INCREASE THE PROSPERITY OF AMERICA'S WORKERS AND EMPLOYERS, THE ECONOMIC GROWTH OF STATES AND REGIONS, AND THE GLOBAL COMPETITIVENESS OF THE UNITED STATES

Innovation is the tool WIBs need to use to engage partners in endeavors of common interest, to solidify their role as system leader, and to add a flavor of excitement and progressiveness to the local system. Here are my 7 suggestions:

- Provide incentives for WIBs to think and operate **regionally**.
- Provide incentives for WIBs to **leverage** their formula allocation for growth.
- Provide incentives for WIBs to create value-added through the **integration** of partner services at the One-Stop level.
- Provide incentives to States to explore a **data-driven** approach to the creation of WIB **catchment** regions.
- Provide incentives for WIBs and States to increase the annual investment in **ITAs** (Individual Training Accounts), both in number and in choice for customers.
- Provide incentives for WIBs to study and determine through analysis the **special populations** that will become central for their work.

- Provide incentives to keep the workforce investment system in a mode of building **capacity** all the time.

4. WHAT WE HAVE DONE TO IMPROVE THE KNOWLEDGE AND SKILLS OF THE NATION'S WORKFORCE . . . WITH FAMILY-SUSTAINING WAGES . . . PARTICULARLY AMERICA'S YOUTH

Go Beyond Formula Funding
- Reliance solely on formula dollars will inhibit ability to become a regional leader and limit ability to serve special populations.
  - With "leveraging" approach, (current budget without ARRA), WorkPlace, Inc. non-formula now 64 percent (1.7 times formula) (i.e. formula is 36 percent of total).
  - Process of leveraging helps to engage partners.
- Particularly as a 501(c)(3) private not-for-profit, WIB has ability to move beyond formula:
  - Actively compete for grants.
  - Solicit money from philanthropic corporate and foundation sources.
  - Create fee-for-service.
- Competitive grants have added to our services, capabilities, and impact.
  - WIRED has enabled us to create partnership with New York (CT–NY Talent for Growth).
  - High-Growth grants supported workforce development in the Advanced Manufacturing and Finance/Insurance sectors.
  - Six grants (multiple sources) built our Disability Services Center in Bridgeport One-Stop, the most comprehensive in the State, and linked to additional services.
  - Five grants in Veterans Services provided intensive training and employment to Homeless and other Veterans.
  - Four grants for Brownfields Environmental Remediation provided technical training and launched graduates into well-paying jobs in promising careers.
  - Total of $50 million over 12 years.

Maximize use of ITA's (Individual Training Accounts)
- Best path to family-sustaining wages is improving skills & knowledge of workers (see "Education Pays" chart from BLS).
  - We make "stretch" commitment to ITA's every year through the budget process.
  - We created privately funded "WorkPlace Scholarships" which have provided training opportunities for more than 1,700 people ($4 million over the past 13 years).

Use a "grow-the-business" model to deliver better services. Here are some of the things we've done at The WorkPlace in line with this model:
- Disability Services Center in One-Stop ("EveryOne Works")
  - Started with competitive grant; when it ended we chose to use WIA $$ to continue staffing. Other grants and State funds have expanded it over time.
  - Voc Rehab partners are engaged (BRS, BESB); we have a common interest in helping people with disabilities get jobs.
- Summer Youth 2009 (ARRA funding)
  - We placed over 700 youth in summer employment, including 24 percent who had certified disabilities.
  - Worked with more than 140 employers (80 private); indemnified them. Our "capacity" helps in having contacts with businesses to place that many in summer jobs.
  - Linked regular WIA-funded youth to summer operations.
- Mortgage Crisis Job Training Program
  - Created a new program in response to growing foreclosures, connecting people to the workforce system to prevent foreclosure and increase their earnings potential.
  - Utilized State funds, in conjunction with leveraging WIA core services (e.g., financial literacy workshops).
- WIRED (CT–NY Talent for Growth)

- We have established cross-state collaborations among training providers, community colleges, economic development, business organizations, and community-based organizations, led by WIBs.
- This initiative has helped us to think from a regional perspective.

SUMMARY

In summary, we are all dedicated to ensuring people who are unemployed get all the services they need, and to serving people in Special Populations. There's a lot of responsibility given to the local delivery system, but WIBs don't carry a big stick—they must earn the respect of their communities and partners. The capacity of WIB's is key to a credible system.

What's needed is to make WIBs a robust enterprise, to grow the business, and to broaden the partnerships. I ask you to look at the local system and give them all the tools they need to make the impact America needs.

Thank you very much for the opportunity to share these thoughts with you.

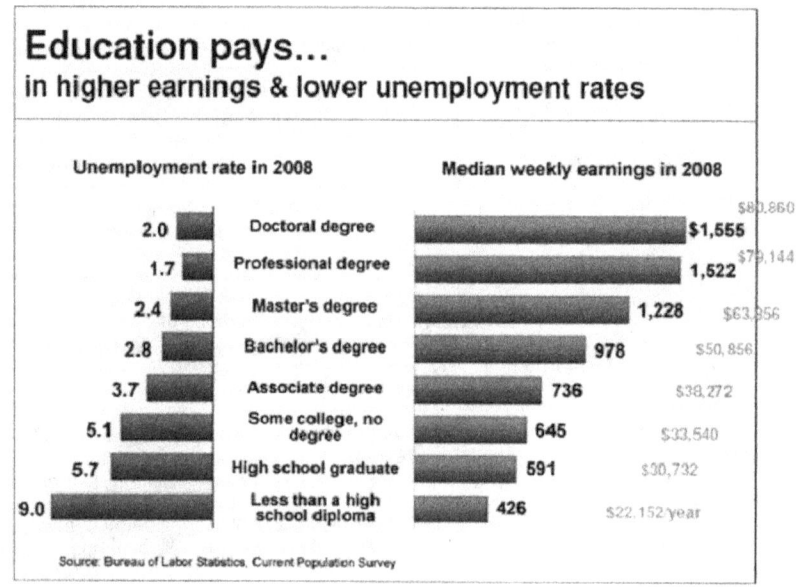

Senator CASEY. Thank you very much.

Mr. Stalknecht.

STATEMENT OF PAUL STALKNECHT, PRESIDENT AND CEO, AIR CONDITIONING CONTRACTORS OF AMERICA, ARLINGTON, VA

Mr. STALKNECHT. Good morning. My name is Paul Stalknecht, and I am the president and chief executive officer of the Air Conditioning Contractors of America. This morning, I will summarize my submitted written testimony.

ACCA serves and represents the small businesses that design, install, and maintain indoor heating, ventilation, air conditioning, and refrigeration, HVACR, systems. Our corporate membership of 4,000 includes more than 3,000 contracting businesses in every State in the country.

I do not profess to be an expert on all the details of the Workforce Investment Act. I can only speak to some concerns and opinions of the industry I represent.

More than half of ACCA's members have fewer than 10 employees. Industry-wide, 60 percent of HVAC contracting firms generate less than $1 million in annual revenue. Yet according to the 2007 Economic Census, altogether we employ nearly 200,000 mechanics, installers, helpers, and related personnel, and these workers have an average salary of approximately $46,500 a year.

Our industry's ability to add skilled employees has not kept up with our overall growth. The problem is going to get worse for us as more building owners and homeowners, fueled by Government incentives and mandates, seek to install new, more energy-efficient heating and cooling systems.

So I ask you, why does an industry that offers good, stable, financially attractive careers—American-made jobs, created by American entrepreneurs, jobs that cannot be shipped overseas— have such a hard time filling these jobs, especially when 30 percent of high school students and 50 percent of minority students still drop out? Something is not clicking.

As the committee considers the reauthorization of the Workforce Investment Act and new directions for the Federal Government's policy for the workforce investment system, allow me to make a few recommendations and observations based on the experiences of ACCA members across the Nation.

First, Congress needs to create Federal policies that change the culture of job training and career counseling. The HVAC industry should be an attractive and rewarding option for those who do not seek a degree beyond secondary school. While you need certain skill levels and a base educational foundation to work in our industry, you do not need a 4-year college degree to get started.

Unfortunately, young people and, to some extent, educators look down on skilled trades that still offer tremendous opportunity, job security, a comfortable lifestyle, and a career path to entrepreneurialism and business ownership. It seems to be a cultural misconnect.

Many business owners in the HVAC industry do not have a 4-year college degree because they started out as a tradesman. As they climbed the career ladder, they learned their business and management skills as they progressed. In contrast, the college-educated business owners who entered the HVAC industry needed to learn their technical skills as they, too, went along. Two different education paths to success, but our society seems to only highlight the college route.

We have seen firsthand the disconnect in workforce development. In our experiences, the limited resources of schools and the perception about work in a "blue collar" field hampers the success of efforts in guiding students to the skilled trades.

Second, on-the-job training must be part of any apprenticeship program in order to be a success. Ours is a technically skilled workforce, and we need to create career paths and opportunities for students and workers. The HVAC industry and other trades require structured education and apprenticeship programs to ensure that our technicians are job-site ready. You simply cannot walk off the street and repair a heating and cooling system.

Community colleges, trade schools, and apprentice programs graduate thousands of students a year, but these programs would

18

work more effectively if the Federal Government made money available to support on-the-job training with local contractors in the trade so trainees can round out their trade skills.

Third, Federal policies should be expanded to encourage and support locally developed and accredited apprenticeship programs that already exist. ACCA's National Capital Chapter in the Washington, DC area oversees a successful apprenticeship program in conjunction with Montgomery Community College and area contractors to train students to be skilled HVAC technicians.

This rigorous 4-year program requires 640 hours of class instruction and 8,000 hours of on-the-job training with a sponsoring employer. With a retention rate of 65 percent, well above the national average of 43 percent, this program has been a tremendous success, graduating some 337 students in the last 18 years.

One common complaint is the Federal and State bureaucracy to start up and administer an apprenticeship program. What is needed is a change in policy to streamline the process for start-up programs and those already in existence. I would ask you to please refer to my submitted comments for a more thorough explanation of my recommendations and comments.

And finally, recognizing some changes need to be made in the workforce investment system philosophically, ACCA and its members support reauthorization of the Workforce Investment Act. With that, I will conclude my comments and would be happy to answer any questions you may have.

Again, thank you for the opportunity to testify before you today.

[The prepared statement of Mr. Stalknecht follows:]

PREPARED STATEMENT OF PAUL STALKNECHT

Good morning. My name is Paul Stalknecht and I am the president and chief executive officer of the Air Conditioning Contractors of America. ACCA is a national trade association with roots extending back to the early part of the 20th century. We serve and represent the small businesses that design, install and maintain indoor heating, ventilation, air conditioning and refrigeration (HVACR) systems. Our corporate membership of 4,000 includes more than 3,000 contracting businesses in every State in the country.

I do not profess to be an expert on all the details of the Workforce Investment Act. I can only speak to some concerns and opinions of the industry I represent.

When I say ACCA represents small businesses, I mean really small businesses. More than half of our members have fewer than 10 employees. Industry-wide, 60 percent of HVACR contracting firms generate less than $1 million in annual revenue.

Yet according to the 2007 Economic Census, altogether we employ nearly 200,000 mechanics, installers, helpers and related personnel, and these workers have an above average salary of $46,500 per employee.

But our industry's ability to add skilled employees has not kept up with our overall growth. Between 2002 and 2007, the value of business performed by HVACR contractors grew 35 percent, but total employees grew only 2 percent.

In fact, prior to the current economic crisis and the fall of the construction market, our industry was faced with a major crisis of its own—a workforce crisis. There simply were not enough *skilled workers* to fill all of the positions available.

The current economic and construction slowdown has eased up on the pressure many contractors have been facing over the last decade. But this is only a temporary stay—and certainly not one that we seek to extend. As the economy improves, we will once again find ourselves with more work than people. The problem is going to get worse for us as more building owners and homeowners, fueled by government incentives and mandates, seek to install new, more energy-efficient heating and cooling systems.

According to the Bureau of Labor Statistics Office of Occupational Statistics and Employment Projections, the need for HVACR mechanics and installers will grow 28 percent between 2008 and 2018.

So I ask you, why does an industry that offers good, stable and financially attractive careers—American-made jobs, created by American entrepreneurs, jobs that cannot be shipped overseas—have such a hard time filling those jobs? Especially when 30 percent of high school students—50 percent of minority students—still drop out? Something is not clicking.

The Federal Government provides funding and resources through the Workforce Investment Act for programs that assist job seekers and employers. Over the last 12 years, the Workforce Investment Act has helped job seekers find the careers that interest them, direct them toward the training they need to be competent in their chosen field so they are attractive to employers, and ultimately connect them with a job. A potential job seeker can find information about a rewarding career path in the HVACR industry and other technical trades using a local One-Stop Career Center or the Department of Labor's *www.careeronestop.org* Web site.

While these programs are helping, ACCA finds that the demand for employees in the technical fields is still not being met, especially given the need for green jobs.

As the committee considers the reauthorization of the Workforce Investment Act and new directions for the Federal Government's policy for the workforce investment system, allow me to make a few recommendations and observations based on the experiences of ACCA members across the Nation.

First, Congress needs to create Federal policies that change the "culture" of job training and career counseling. The HVACR industry should be an attractive and rewarding option for those who do not seek a degree beyond secondary school. While you need certain skill levels and a base educational foundation to work in the HVACR industry, you don't need a 4-year college degree. In the last few decades, it seems our society has denigrated the skilled trades in favor of 4-year colleges. Government policy and cultural shifts have created a world where young people "look down" on the skilled trades that still offer tremendous opportunity, job security, a comfortable lifestyle, and a career path to entrepreneurialism and business ownership.

According to the BLS, only 16.4 percent of workers employed as HVACR technicians and installers between the ages of 25 and 44 hold an associate's degree, bachelor's degree or higher. Overall, nearly 27 percent of workers between the ages of 25 and 44 employed in the HVACR industry have attended some college without graduating.

Many business owners in the HVACR industry do not have a 4-year college degree. They started out as tradesmen—some perhaps getting their start through a Workforce Investment Act program (or one of its predecessors). As they climbed the career ladder, they learned their business and management skills on the fly. In contrast, the college educated business owners who entered the HVACR industry needed to learn their technical skills as they went along. Two different education paths to success, but our society seems only to highlight the college route.

There are students with no interest in a 4-year degree who are being pushed to attend one anyway. They take on debt they don't want so that they can get a job they don't want which often pays less than they would have been making after 4 years of working in the HVACR industry.

And there are students so disillusioned by our educational system that they drop out of it altogether. High school dropouts still make up an alarming percentage of our children, nearly 30 percent. It does not appear that we are doing all that we can, as a society, to help our young people identify their strengths and the right career paths they should take to exploit them.

Members of ACCA's Michigan chapter have first-hand experience with this disconnect in workforce development. Some of our contractor members in Michigan have taken a proactive approach by working with teachers and guidance counselors, getting on curriculum planning committees and school boards, and participating in job fairs. In their experiences, the limited resources of schools and the perception about work in a "blue collar" field hampered the success of their efforts. This culture and attitude needs to change.

Second, on-the-job training must be part of any apprenticeship program in order to be a success. Ours is a technically skilled workforce and we need to create career paths and opportunities for students and workers to gain entry into the good-paying green collar jobs offered by the HVACR industry and other skilled trades. Work in the HVACR industry requires structured education and apprenticeship programs to ensure that our technicians are able to do the job and do it right. You can't just walk in off the street and repair a heating or cooling system, which is why on-the-job training must be a key component to training.

Community colleges, trade schools, and apprenticeship programs graduate students but in many cases they lack specific skills because they didn't have on-the-job training. These programs would work more effectively if the Federal Government made money available to support on-the-job training with local contractors in the trade so trainees can round out their skill sets.

Programs developed at the State and local levels through the Workforce Investment Boards should emphasize on-the-job training as part of any job training program. It boosts the confidence of the employee and it helps establish a better educational foundation to build one's career.

Third, Federal policies should be expanded to encourage and support locally developed and accredited apprenticeship programs that already exist. ACCA's National Capital Chapter in the Washington, DC area oversees a successful apprenticeship program in conjunction with Montgomery Community College and area contractors to train students to be skilled HVACR technicians. This 4-year program requires 640 hours of class instruction and 8,000 hours of on-the-job training with a sponsoring employer. Class sizes range from 32 to 41 students, with a retention rate of 65 percent—well above the national average of 43 percent for a similar program. Since 1992, the apprenticeship program has graduated 337 students. Upon graduation, participants receive a recognized certificate and earn credits toward an associate's degree. And they are able to apply for their Journeyman's license without taking the State exam.

One common complaint by program administrators is compliance with Federal paper work and recordkeeping requirements for certification. Apprenticeship program administrators must jump through many bureaucratic hoops to gain approval from State and Federal agencies, including the Department of Labor and the Veterans Administration. What's needed is a change in policy to streamline the process for start up programs and those already in existence.

Fourth, Congress should continue to support and expand the roles of the Workforce Investment Boards across the country. Workforce Investment Boards work best because they involve local business leaders along with representatives from schools and trades. Unfortunately on many boards, the 51 percent business majority is theoretical with many meetings having few business attendees. Therefore, to ensure that business engagement occurs at each meeting, we recommend that a quorum of business people must be present. In addition, the composition of these boards should be modified to reduce the number of federally mandated partners while still ensuring the voices of all stakeholders are heard. These business-majority boards should provide general oversight of the local system including oversight of the One-Stop Career Centers and provide a forum for coordination among various agencies and organizations.

Finally, I urge you to consider assisting small businesses that develop their own in-house training. Several ACCA member companies that qualify as small businesses have created their own apprenticeship programs with rigorous standards that are recognized by the Department of Labor. These are especially critical in rural areas where trainees may find limited options for training.

For example, ACCA member company Service Legends of Des Moines, IA, developed an apprenticeship program approved by the Department of Labor that trains employees from the ground up. Interest is so great that Service Legends receives 120 applicants per month as job seekers aim to join their team.

Improving our Nation's workforce investment system is a complicated but necessary effort. Our economy needs a continuous supply of highly skilled workers to expand. I know that high school guidance counselors are overworked, underpaid, and often uninformed about the value of skilled trade careers. Perhaps in larger high schools, or high schools with an unusually high drop-out rate, at least one guidance counselor should become proficient in technical trade opportunities and assigned to *only* handle technical trades placements.

ACCA's member companies are the foot soldiers in the new movement to install and service energy efficient infrastructure in American homes and buildings. If our economy is to grow, employers will need a steady stream of qualified applicants to replace employees lost to attrition and fulfill the expected needs of the future.

With that I will conclude my comments and would be happy to answer any questions you may have. Thank you again for this opportunity to testify before you.

Senator CASEY. Well, thank you very much.

Ms. Feldman, I was handed a note that said that you got 10 stitches in your forehead last night?

Ms. FELDMAN. Yes.

Senator CASEY. Well, then——

Ms. FELDMAN. I would like to give a shout-out actually to the emergency room team at George Washington University Hospital. They did a great job.

[Laughter.]

Senator CASEY. Well, you can take a half an hour for your statement if you would like.

[Laughter.]

STATEMENT OF CHERYL FELDMAN, EXECUTIVE DIRECTOR, DISTRICT 1199C TRAINING AND UPGRADING FUND, PHILADELPHIA, PA

Ms. FELDMAN. Thank you for inviting me today.

My name is Cheryl Feldman. I am director of District 1199C Training and Upgrading Fund in your fair city of Philadelphia. The fund is a labor-management partnership of 49 area healthcare employers in Philadelphia and South Jersey and the AFSCME-affiliated National Union of Hospital and Health Care Employees. Accompanying me today is the president of our union, Henry Nicholas.

Senator CASEY. You now have more time.

[Laughter.]

Ms. FELDMAN. I thank you for this opportunity.

I only have limited time. I only can tell you about a portion of our work. My main point is that we are uniquely situated within our industry, as a labor-management partnership, to bring together public programs, private sector firms, and private industry dollars to solve our healthcare workforce challenges.

We use WIA title I funds to train workers, title II funds to teach workers reading and writing and math for the workplace, and TANF dollars to help low-income women get on a career path. We work with local universities and community colleges and local employers to help healthcare workers get time off to attend specially designed credit-bearing programs that lead to college degrees. We work with youth to interest them in health careers and incumbent workers already in the industry who are looking for new options for advancement.

The State and local WIA job training system and literacy system are indispensable partners for us. Federal WIA policies could make our balancing act much easier if they didn't create the silos, the barriers against aligning adult basic ed with technical training, with public assistance, with work supports, with work release programs. It is a lot to manage.

Due to State budget cuts in Pennsylvania, our workforce literacy program has been cut by 30 percent. We have 400 people on a waiting list right now. If there weren't the silos, we could blend our literacy and workforce programs together and get those folks started in healthcare careers.

WIA could make a much greater investment in sector strategies such as ours, much as our State has done through its industry partnership initiatives. Ultimately, WIA needs to be much better funded to help programs like ours grow and serve the larger number of workers and employers seeking our services.

Our labor-management fund offers a powerful solution to Philadelphia's challenges because we simultaneously address the skill needs of low-income workers and the talent needs of our regional businesses. Our partnership brings together multiple employers in the same industry to identify talent gaps. Then we help prepare the low-skilled adults to fill these available, mid-skilled positions, which are still available in healthcare.

This sector approach builds on the mutual interest that the employers and the workers have and provides an excellent example of the innovative "industry partnership" model through our Pennsylvania Department of Labor and Industry. Thanks to our State leadership, there are now more than 70 industry-led partnerships in Pennsylvania that are similar to ours that engage 6,300 businesses and help to train more than 75,000 workers.

An example—Elizabeth Vasquez. At 19, she enrolled in our TANF-funded nurse aide training program, and you spoke at her graduation, Senator Casey. Upon completion, she obtained a unionized nurse aide job.

Because her employer contributed 1.5 percent of gross payroll through its collective bargaining agreement, Elizabeth had access to the Training Fund's education benefits, and so she went to practical nursing and tripled her wages. Now she is completing a registered nursing program in three semesters as a result of our LPN to RN articulation with the community college.

Our Jobs to Careers Behavioral Health Program, working with incumbent workers, we have done a little bit about what Tony Carnevale said. We have embedded the training in the workplace so that there is a combination of traditional classroom hours and on-the-job learning assignments. Students get 21 college credits for this work. It articulates directly into an associate and then a bachelor's degree.

The program speaks for itself. We have had 100 percent of the graduates receive wage increases, with promotions in some cases. Many are now in college, and new employers are implementing this innovative program.

By leveraging public and private funding, the fund's labor-management partnership has helped over 100,000 workers in our 35 years. And we are not alone. Other labor-management partnerships in healthcare and other industries are engaged in equally compelling work.

I would like to emphasize that with long-term resources, which is what we need, we can replicate innovative and sustainable workforce initiatives that prepare adults and youth with the skills to compete in the global economy.

I thank you so much for having me today.

[The prepared statement of Ms. Feldman follows:]

PREPARED STATEMENT OF CHERYL FELDMAN

Chairman Harkin and honorable members of the committee, thank you for inviting me to participate in today's hearing. My name is Cheryl Feldman and I am Director of the District 1199C Training & Upgrading Fund. The Fund is a labor management partnership of 49 Philadelphia area and South Jersey healthcare employers and the AFSCME-affiliated National Union of Hospital and Health Care Employees. I thank you for the honor and the opportunity to share our experience in creating a workforce strategy that integrates education and training with career pathways linked to quality jobs.

With limited time, I can only tell you about a portion of the work we do with a wide range of healthcare workers and employers. My written testimony will go into more detail. But, my main point to be made today is that we are uniquely situated within our industry, as a labor-management partnership, to bring together a wide range of public programs, private-sector firms, and private industry dollars to help solve our city's healthcare workforce challenges. We use WIA title I funds to train workers, WIA title II funds to teach workers reading, writing, and math skills needed in the workplace, and TANF dollars to help low-income women get on a career path. We work with local universities and local employers to help healthcare workers get time off to attend specially designed credit-bearing programs that lead to college degrees. We work with youth to interest them in health careers, and we work with incumbent workers already in the industry who are looking for new options for advancement.

The State and local WIA title I job training system and title II literacy system are indispensable partners. But Federal WIA policies could make our balancing act much easier if they did not create barriers against aligning adult basic education, technical training, public assistance, work supports and work release for workers in our industry. Due to State budget cuts in Pennsylvania, our workforce literacy program has been cut by 30 percent resulting in a waiting list of over 400 applicants wanting to come in our program. Without the existing silos, we could potentially enroll some of those on the waiting list in blended literacy-skills training programs and get them started in healthcare careers.

WIA could make a much greater investment in sector strategies such as ours, much as our State has already done through its Industry Partnership program. And, ultimately, WIA needs to be much better funded, to help programs like ours grow and serve the larger number of workers and employers who are seeking our services.

Our Fund in 1974 began with 15 hospital service workers in a GED class held around a folding table in the union hall. Today, we host a fully-equipped learning center in the heart of downtown Philadelphia and satellite locations in the region that educate 3,200 youth and adult students annually. We have opened doors to career advancement and prepared students to play a role in the healthcare workplace of the future with GED, literacy, skills training, college preparatory and degree programs. We also provide 18,000 Philadelphia area community residents with a variety of services, including testing for healthcare credentials, GED testing, VITA tax preparation, job placement services, academic assessments, and career counseling.

Philadelphia is currently experiencing parallel workforce crises: employers in the region lack a strong talent pipeline to fill critical jobs, while an alarmingly high percentage of adults are in the labor force only marginally or not at all. Indeed, 70 percent of jobs in our city require basic literacy skills, but less than 50 percent of our residents possess these minimum skills. Healthcare is no exception. Our industry, comprising 15 percent of Philadelphia's economy, is showing growth during the recession but the new jobs require literate, trained workers.

Our Fund offers a powerful solution to Philadelphia's challenges by simultaneously addressing the skill needs of low-income workers and the talent needs of regional businesses. Our partnership brings together multiple employers in the same industry to identify talent gaps. Then, we help prepare low-skilled adults to fill these available, mid-skilled positions. This sector approach builds on the mutual interest of employers and workers, and provides an excellent example of the innovative "industry partnership" model that the Pennsylvania Department of Labor & Industry has launched statewide. Thanks to State leadership, there are now more than 70 industry-led partnerships similar to ours, engaging more than 6,300 businesses and helping to train more than 75,000 workers.

In the 35 years since the Fund was created, this unique collaboration of employers and labor has never once reached an impasse. We have built a strong alliance that is able to assess the rapidly evolving needs of today's healthcare workplace with labor market data provided by the Pennsylvania Center for Health Careers and the State workforce system. In response to the nursing shortage of the late 1990's, we leveraged H–1B funding with Training Fund and employer dollars to train 1,700 nurses and allied health staff in partnership with area schools. We called this initiative the New Faces Program, encouraging non-traditional students, immigrants, and youth to take advantage of the shortage to enter a healthcare career. As hospitals move toward adoption of Electronic Health Records, we are engaged in proactive discussions about how best to prepare frontline healthcare and clerical workers to expand their technology skills.

The trajectory of Elizabeth Vasquez exemplifies how programs that address employers' workforce needs also benefit individuals. At 19, Elizabeth enrolled in our TANF funded Nurse Aide training program. Upon completion, she obtained a unionized Nurse Aide job. Because her employer contributed 1.5 percent of gross payroll through its collective bargaining agreement, Elizabeth had access to the Training

Fund's educational benefits to train as a Practical Nurse, tripling her hourly wages. Elizabeth is now completing a Registered Nursing Program in three semesters as a result of Training Fund and State Industry Partnership funding which helped create an LPN to RN Articulation Program.

Our Jobs to Careers Program uses innovative best practices to retool and advance incumbent workers along a career pathway. Job competencies are embedded in a work-based curriculum that replaces traditional classroom hours with on-the-job learning assignments. An accelerated literacy component ensures academic success. Cohorts of workers attend the program together on release time from their job, receiving support from peers, supervisors, and a Career Coach. Twenty-one college credits, articulating with Associate's and Bachelor's Degrees, are awarded for completion of the technical training. The outcomes speak for themselves. One hundred percent of the graduates have received wage increases with promotions in some cases, many are now college students, and new employers are implementing the program.

As a member of the Philadelphia Youth Council, I am delighted that we are investing in our future healthcare workers by expanding youth pipeline programs. Subsidized employment is making it possible for healthcare employers to open their doors to young workers in internships and supported work programs with opportunities to transition into unsubsidized jobs. ARRA funding is providing the opportunity to create innovative industry pipeline programs for in-school youth and GED to college programs for out-of-school youth. By allowing alternative eligibility criteria for WIA funding we will ensure that even more disadvantaged youth can participate.

By leveraging public and private funding, the Fund's labor management partnership has helped over 100,000 workers secure and advance in careers with family sustaining wages. We are not alone. Other labor management partnerships in healthcare and other industries are engaged in equally compelling work. We can build greater capacity with dedicated workforce and literacy funding for sector work as part of the national workforce development system. With long-term resources, we can replicate innovative and sustainable workforce initiatives that prepare adults and youth with the skills to compete in the global economy.

Thank you very much for the opportunity to speak today.

————

ATTACHMENT—DISTRICT 1199C TRAINING & UPGRADING FUND: HELPING TODAY'S HEALTHCARE WORKERS PREPARE FOR TOMORROW'S WORKPLACE*

THE HISTORY

The District 1199C Training & Upgrading Fund has played a critical role in offering academic, career exposure and workforce development opportunities to youth and adults in Philadelphia for 35 years. Tomorrow's healthcare needs drive our training and education agenda. Occupational projections from the Bureau of Labor Statistics indicate that within the next decade, 45 percent of the jobs will require a post-secondary credential compared with only 25 percent today. In addition to our current offerings, we are preparing for future jobs such as health information technology and preparing future workers by, for example, strengthening the youth pipeline into entry level healthcare careers.

THE HIGHLIGHTS

Scope of Service: Providing Career Pathways in Healthcare

In fiscal year 2009, we served a total of 17,856 people. The Fund's expansive offerings include programs in nursing, allied health, behavioral health, computer technology, college prep and collegiate partnerships programs. We provide a variety of services including American Red Cross Nurse Aide testing, VITA tax preparation, job placement services, academic assessment services and healthcare career exposure workshops. The Fund offers a part-time practical nursing program designed for working people. Half of the students of District 1199C Training & Upgrading Fund are members of the Training Fund and half are community residents—dislocated and unemployed workers as well as immigrants.

————

*The District 1199C Training & Upgrading Fund is a Labor-Management Partnership dedicated to providing access to healthcare employment for current and future workers while also serving the educational and training needs of our Delaware Valley healthcare employers.

Employer Engagement: Meeting Employer Needs for a Qualified Workforce

We are the educational arm of our 49 employer partners. The Fund has multi-employer sector initiatives including customized career advancement training for entry-level workers, licensure and certification review classes and skills-based classes that support the delivery of quality care. Temple University Health Systems has co-chaired the Fund's Board of Directors for 20 years.

Adult Academic Readiness Services: Accelerating Transition to Post-Secondary Education

In fiscal year 2009, we provided educational services to 3,200 students. Our programs range from GED/Adult Diploma programs to healthcare contextualized English, mathematics and ESL classes as well as a variety of technical training programs resulting in an industry-recognized credential that articulates with college credits and degree programs. We provide blended preparatory and technical bridge curricula that enable students to accelerate learning and successfully transition into post-secondary.

Youth Pipeline Services: Preparing the Future Workforce

The Fund offers a variety of programs that serve close to 400 youth annually. We have partnered with the School District of Philadelphia and Philadelphia Academies for 15 years to host a Health Career Day targeting 10th–12th graders, exposing them to healthcare careers, and for the past 2 years we have sponsored Job Shadowing Day for high school students. In partnership with the Philadelphia Youth Network, we also offer the Summer Health Exploration Program, the GED to College Program, the Nurse Aide Training for Out-of-School Youth Program and the 21st Century Continuum Program for 11th and 12th graders at Lincoln High School, a collaboration of the Philadelphia Academies Inc., Community College of Philadelphia, Children's Hospital of Philadelphia and the Fund.

Career Pathways Counseling & Placement: Offering Supportive Services

The Fund provides comprehensive coaching to support students in achieving their career advancement goals. A career counselor helps individuals create an individual educational plan as well as help individuals with resume development, interviewing skills, and job placement.

Funding

In fiscal year 2009, the Fund leveraged $2.8 million. We were awarded public and foundation grants from 16 organizations to enhance programs and expand our services. Our funders include the National Fund for Workforce Solutions, the U.S. Department of Labor, the Pennsylvania Departments of Labor and Industry and of Education, the city of Philadelphia, the Robert Wood Johnson Foundation, the Hitachi Foundation, the Knight Foundation, the William Penn Foundation, the Annie E. Casey Foundation and United Way of southeastern Pennsylvania.

THE COLLABORATIONS

- Pennsylvania Center for Health Careers
- Philadelphia Council for College and Career Success
- Life Science Career Alliance
- Philadelphia Academies Inc.
- School District of Philadelphia's Perkins Advisory Council
- Citywide Health and Life Sciences Advisory Council
- Workforce Solutions Collaborative
- Careerlink Philadelphia North Advisory Committee
- National Network of Sector Partners
- The National Skills Coalition
- President's Economic Recovery Advisory Board *Education & Training Subcommittee Healthcare Workforce Meeting*

EDUCATION WORKS

EDUCATIONAL AND CAREER ADVANCEMENT PROGRAMS IN HEALTHCARE CHANGE LIVES AND IMPROVE PATIENT CARE AND PREPARE EMPLOYEES FOR TOMORROW'S WORKPLACE

In Healthcare Today, Every Employee Counts

Delivering top-quality healthcare while remaining financially sound has never been easy. But today's healthcare providers face greater challenges than ever before:

- Severe shortages and high turnover of nurses, allied health professionals and direct care workers;

- Competition from new forms of healthcare delivery;
- Constant demands to update technology and equipment; and
- Steep cuts in governmental funding.

To survive and thrive, successful healthcare organizations must find cost-effective ways to prepare employees for a more complex, demanding workplace. At a time when providers must do more with less, the skill level of every employee counts.

Education Works—for the Entire Organization

Employee educational and career advancement programs strengthen the organization's ability to:

- Prepare for changes that are constantly reshaping healthcare practice and policy;
- Maximize the knowledge and skills of those already on the job;
- Create life-changing opportunities, particularly for workers in low-wage, low-skill positions;
- Reduce the high cost of turnover by retaining skilled workers; and
- Attract workers trained to meet the needs of your organization.

As employees advance, so does the entire organization. Workers gain greater skill, job satisfaction, career advancement—and the ability to deliver better quality patient care.

Providing "Industry-Specific" Training to Healthcare Providers

Because they are based on the challenges employees face every day, "industry-specific" educational programs achieve greater lasting benefits for employers and employees than general academic programs. In the Philadelphia region, the **District 1199C Training & Upgrading Fund** is one of the leading providers of educational and training programs specifically tailored to employees in the healthcare industry.

Opening Doors to Life-Changing Opportunities

Every year, nearly 5,000 employees enroll in training and educational programs offered by the Training Fund at the Breslin Learning Center and area schools of nursing and allied health. These students are a vital asset to their employers and enjoy the benefits of greater job satisfaction, higher wages and the opportunity to contribute to the quality of care in their organization.

PROVIDING VITAL EDUCATIONAL RESOURCES FOR THE HEALTHCARE PROVIDERS
IN THE PHILADELPHIA REGION

The Training Fund—Partnering With 54 Regional Healthcare and Human Services Employers

Because most healthcare employers do not have the time or resources to develop full-service educational programs of their own, a unique collaboration was formed between District 1199C and healthcare providers in southeastern Pennsylvania and southern New Jersey. Since 1974, this educational partnership has:

- Improved patient care;
- Helped thousands of employees move up the career ladder while on the job;
- Boosted employer recruitment and retention efforts;
- Attracted new workers to the healthcare field; and
- Enabled employers to build a more skilled, diverse workforce.

The Training Fund is a jointly managed, non-profit trust of District 1199C of the National Union of Hospital & Healthcare Employees, AFSCME and 54 healthcare employers in the Philadelphia region. The Fund serves more than 17,000 Delaware Valley residents annually.

Providing Vital Resources to the Region's Healthcare Employers

The Training Fund helps regional healthcare providers gain access to valuable expertise and resources through its network of governmental agencies, labor and business organizations, grass-roots community-based organizations, foundations, area colleges and universities, the School District of Philadelphia and the William Penn School District in Delaware County. These links enable the Training Fund to take a leading role in shaping healthcare policy and practice, to collaborate on new initiatives and to keep employers and workers current with changes in the field.

The U.S. Department of Labor and the PA Department of Labor and Industry have awarded the Training Fund millions of dollars in Federal and State grants for nursing and allied health programs. The Training Fund has been recognized as a national model for its innovative programs in healthcare career advancement.

A One-Stop Resource for Health Career Training

At the Fund's spacious, well-equipped Center City Philadelphia location, at satellite centers in the region or customized programs at your worksite, the Training Fund offers a wide range of programs, including:

Basic Academic Preparation
- Basic education, literacy and English as a Second Language (ESL) programs;
- Tuition-free, self-paced adult high school diploma program;
- GED preparation;
- Pre-college academic enrichment/preparation for higher education;
- Pre-nursing programs; and
- IC3 Certification in Microsoft Word, Excel and Internet computing.

Professional Programs in Healthcare and Human Services
- Nurse Aide and Extended Nursing Duties;
- Licensed Practical Nurse (LPN);
- Funding for Associate, Bachelor, Registered Nurse, and Allied Health degrees;
- Behavioral Health College Program;
- Child Development;
- Allied Health Technical Programs; and
- Health Information Technology.

Flexible, Part-Time Collegiate Programs Leading to Degrees
- **Articulation of the Training Fund's Practical Nursing Program** (LPN) with the Registered Nursing Program of Community College of Philadelphia (Under development).
- **30-credit certificate and 60-credit Associate Degree program in Behavioral Health** offered at the Training Fund. This program articulates with Philadelphia University's Behavioral Health and Human Services bachelor's degree program.
- **Philadelphia University Prerequisite Courses for Nursing and Allied Health.** College-level credit prerequisites are now offered at the Breslin Learning Center in collaboration with Philadelphia University—in flexible evening, morning, and weekend formats.

Workforce Development and Employment Services

The Training Fund Placement Service works with more than 100 healthcare facilities to refer pre-screened, qualified job candidates, including program graduates, new entrants to health-care and experienced employees looking to advance in their field.

Customized Educational and Organizational Development Programs

Training Fund staff also work with employers to create customized solutions for specific educational or training objectives, based on the needs of the organization and skill levels of the employees. These have included: specialty skills training to fulfill mandated insurance regulations; pre-nursing/pre-allied health; effective communication skills; multi-cultural and cross-cultural understanding; English as a Second Language (ESL) and basic foundation skills in reading, writing and mathematics; conflict management; mentoring training for frontline direct care workers and job coach training for their supervisors.

helping healthcare workers advance up the career ladder

Helping Employees Pursue Their Education While on the Job

Juggling full-time jobs and family responsibilities can make it challenging for many adults to re-enter the classroom. The Training Fund helps ease the transition through a range of services: confidential academic and vocational counseling, academic and career interest assessments, and assistance with resume writing, interviewing and job search. While in the program, participants receive mentoring from Training Fund faculty and staff to encourage, motivate and guide them toward their educational and career goals.

Flexible Scheduling Helps Everyone Succeed

To help insure the success of full-time employees attending training programs, the Fund works with employers to offer release-time programs, either on or off the clock. Working adults can choose from among flexible, part-time programs, offered 7 days a week in two shifts.

Offering Many Convenient Locations

Students may attend educational programs at:
• The Training Fund's Thomas Breslin Learning Center in downtown Philadelphia;
  • Our satellite location in Cherry Hill, NJ; and
  • Customized career ladder programs at the employer's workplace.

Full Educational and Financial Benefits for Partnering Employers

Employers who contribute to the District 1199C Training Fund can obtain the highest level of education and training benefits for their employees. Government funding obtained by the Training Fund helps employers leverage their training investment and expand opportunities for member employees, who are eligible for three levels of educational funding support:
• **Tuition reimbursement** up to $5,000 per year for approved courses, workshops, seminars and conferences at area colleges, universities and vocational programs as well as programs by accrediting organizations.
• **Full-time scholarships** covering tuition up to $10,000 per year for up to 2 years of study.
• **Free continuing education programs** with flexible (day, evening and weekend) schedules at the Breslin Learning Center and satellite locations. Many classes are open to community members, as well as union members.

Healthcare Training Programs Open to Community Members

Community members who wish to attend programs at the Training Fund, or healthcare employees who are not covered by the educational benefit may pursue educational programs at the Training Fund at a non-profit tuition rate, or may be eligible for free training through a range of government programs.

TRANSFORMING PHILADELPHIA'S HEALTHCARE WORKFORCE

Creating a Pipeline for New Healthcare Workers

As the healthcare industry copes with a severe shortage of qualified workers, the Training Fund is helping employers by creating a pipeline to new employees. By virtue of its credibility and well-established reputation in the community, the Training Fund successfully attracts incumbent workers, minorities, immigrants and young people into the field of healthcare, and provides employers with greater access to a more diverse, skilled workforce.

Preparing Youth for Careers in Healthcare

The Training Fund has partnered with the School District of Philadelphia through its health-care academies and Citywide Health Advisory Council, as well as with the Philadelphia Youth Network to create high-quality secondary school curricula and work-based learning opportunities for youth interested in careers in healthcare. The Training Fund has led efforts to draw more in-school and out-of-school youth to careers in the healthcare field and better prepare them to pursue higher education and professional careers.

Designing Career Ladders for Other Settings and Industries

As healthcare delivery has changed, the Training Fund's educational offerings have moved beyond hospitals to include long-term care facilities, mental health and retardation programs, home care and community-based agencies. In addition, the Training Fund develops educational programs for other industries to enable workers to move up the career ladder within their particular organization. The Fund works with employers to integrate instructions in reading, writing, math, and ESL with the specific work skills needed on the job. Examples include transit workers, parking facility attendants and university dining service employees.

For More Information:

The District 1199C Training & Upgrading Fund provides significant employee benefits to member agencies. If you need more information about the work of the Training Fund, please contact us at:

District 1199C Training & Upgrading Fund: 1319 Locust Street, Philadelphia, PA 19107, (215) 735–555 (voice); (215) 735–7910 (fax).

Thomas Breslin Learning Center: 100 South Broad Street, 10th Floor, Philadelphia, PA 19110, (215) 568–2220 (voice); (215) 563–4683 (fax).

District 1199C South Jersey Office: 401 Route 70 East, Cherry Hill, NJ 08034, (856) 428–8355 (voice); (856) 428–6705 (fax).

Web site: www.1199ctraining.org.

E-mail: mail@1199ctraining.org.

Senator CASEY. Thank you very much, Ms. Feldman.

Mr. Templin.

STATEMENT OF ROBERT TEMPLIN, JR., PRESIDENT, NORTHERN VIRGINIA COMMUNITY COLLEGE (NOVA), ANNANDALE, VA

Mr. TEMPLIN. Mr. Chairman, members of the committee, thank you very much for having me today.

My name is Bob Templin. I am the president of Northern Virginia Community College, or what we call NOVA, and we have 72,000 students enrolled in post-secondary education, most often leading to a credential that is valuable in the workplace.

In addition, we train over 20,000 workers annually, and we are one of the largest and most ethnically diverse institutions of higher education in America. We are only 1 out of nearly 1,200 community colleges across the country, and we represent 44 percent of the Nation's undergraduate students that are enrolled today. That is about 7 million students that are in credit programs and another 5 million that are in the workforce.

I am going to try to connect the dots of what we have been talking about today, that as the economy begins to grow and jobs are created, the jobs with the greatest livable wage, with the greatest opportunity, are going to be middle-tier jobs that require more education than high school, but not necessarily the baccalaureate.

Under our current programs, often we are encouraged to develop through community-based organizations job training programs that lead to entry-level jobs, and that is great. That is not sufficient. Low-wage earners who get entry-level jobs without a post-secondary credential will be the first laid off when the economy turns down or there is a change in technology.

We have to connect WIA-funded programs to encourage individuals to continue their education to accomplish a post-secondary degree. It needs to be an explicit component.

Now that post-secondary credential doesn't have to be a college degree. It can be an industry certification. It can be completion of apprenticeship. Too often we allow individuals to stop at the very moment they begin to experience success. We have to explicitly link and encourage innovation between players in the WIA system and measure their performance and accountability against results of their clients receiving post-secondary credentials.

If we can do that linkage, we can pull people out of poverty and into family-sustainable wage jobs. In my testimony, I have given three examples of how that could be done. One of them is a program that NOVA operates with a comprehensive social service organization that helps families in poverty. Most of them are immigrant.

That program prepares individuals to do entry-level office work using Microsoft Office software, to serve as receptionists and administrative assistants in medical offices. When they complete that program, because of the linkage that it has with NOVA, they have completed almost one semester of college credit.

Their employers agree when they hire them to encourage them to continue their education toward an associate degree, and they help reimburse tuition for that expense. As a consequence, almost half of the graduates from the community-based program receive an entry-level job and then continue their education toward a credential.

They have a future. They will have a stackable, portable credential that, in the event that they are laid off, they will have a credential that they can go to another employer and receive a job.

A second example is in an area for youngsters who have graduated from high school, but have no plan. Perhaps no one in their family ever went to college. They don't know what careers are available and what to do. Northern Virginia Community College created a link with a community-based organization called Year Up.

That Year Up provides classroom instruction for about 6 months with a paid wage and then an apprenticeship. The students don't think they are going to college, but when they complete that program, they have skills for an entry-level job and 18 college credits through Northern Virginia Community College and an employer that insists that they continue their education toward an associate degree.

Once again, a person moving at the IT help desk level has a wage but, without a credential, has no chance of progressing. With an associate degree, they have a future, a portable degree, and the opportunity to continue their education at a university.

A third example fits right into the disabled community that the chairman spoke about earlier. Imagine for a moment, Goodwill Industries International has 180 regional offices across the United States helping the disabled to get entry-level skills, and that is wonderful. What would happen is—those 180 regional offices connected with America's 1,200 community colleges and created the option for college credit for them to get the skills, get the credit, and then continue their education and to have a career opportunity.

WIA reauthorization needs to encourage collaboration across sectors and put a premium on the achievement of post-secondary market-valued credentials.

Thank you very much, Mr. Chairman.

[The prepared statement of Mr. Templin follows:]

PREPARED STATEMENT OF ROBERT G. TEMPLIN, JR.*

Chairman Harkin, Ranking Member Enzi, and distinguished members of the committee, thank you for the opportunity to address you today. My name is Bob Templin and I am the president of Northern Virginia Community College, or "NOVA" as our students call us. NOVA is an open door, public community college offering credit programs through the associate degree level, as well as workforce development programs. Serving over 72,000 students annually in degree credit programs and 20,000 in workforce development courses, NOVA is one of the largest and most ethnically diverse institutions of higher education in the United States.

I have come to speak with you today about the need for our Nation to create an integrated workforce development system that offers a seamless delivery of services to address employment, education, and skill needs of workers, job seekers, and employers.

---

*Note: Portions of this testimony are excerpts or adaptations of the American Association of Community College's white paper entitled, "AACC WIA Reauthorization Priorities." However, this testimony does not necessarily reflect the entire or official position of AACC.

THE NEXT ECONOMIC RECOVERY: WHO WILL BENEFIT?

Even as the unsettled economy continues to behave in volatile ways, forecasters are predicting that a new generation of innovations (from energy, the life sciences, green technologies, health care reform, and information technology) hold the promise not only of driving economic recovery, but also of sparking another extended period of economic expansion in America. If such forecasts are on target, there will be many opportunities for those who are ready to take advantage of the economic updrafts. But during the last economic expansion, too many poor Americans did not gain lift from these updrafts. During the next economic expansion, our country must take the initiative, anticipate labor market changes before or as they occur, and then use these changes to create new economic opportunities for all of our people, including those from low-income neighborhoods. What should our country be doing now that will help our poor people and low-income communities soar when the economy rises again?

Even when skill shortages re-emerge, adults and youth living in low-income communities are likely to be left out of the picture, unless special efforts are made. They not only lack the specific skill sets required for the changing economy, they often lack the foundational knowledge needed to acquire higher-level skills, and they most often lack a market-valued portable credential. The poor frequently are the last to benefit from economic expansion and among the first to be affected by downturns in the economy such as the current recession. Entry-level skill training represents only one part of what is required for a worker to secure and retain meaningful employment. Without broader foundational knowledge, post-secondary level training, a portable credential, and actual job experience, narrowly focused skill development too often results in a one-way ticket to entry level jobs that are the first to be lost at the next technology innovation or economic downturn.

BUILDING A WORKFORCE SYSTEM WITH FAMILY-SUSTAINING WAGES

The challenge is that we have to move beyond a preoccupation with short-term entry-level skills training and move toward a workforce development system that encourages training that leads to both employment and a post-secondary credential and provides employment with family-sustaining wages.

In reauthorizing the Workforce Investment Act (WIA), Congress should reform the workforce system with the goal of providing workers access not only to immediate employment, but simultaneous access to portable and "stackable" post-secondary credentials leading to sustainable-wage jobs. Currently, WIA and other workforce development programs are not doing enough to establish clear and multiple pathways to market-valued post-secondary credentials for workers, especially those with low-skill levels. Too often training providers operate in relative isolation providing entry-level training skills that do not result in a portable and market-valued credential. And, they are not incentivized to work as part of a larger workforce system, across organizational boundaries, to create a seamless pipeline that develops low-skill individuals into higher-skill workers who can find and maintain employment in higher-wage jobs. To do this, the workforce investment system must spur greater degrees of innovation and collaboration between key stakeholders.

THE ROLE OF AMERICA'S COMMUNITY COLLEGES IN THE NEW WORKFORCE SYSTEM

One of those key stakeholders is America's community colleges. With the proposed American Graduation Initiative (AGI), the current Administration has recognized the importance of community colleges in making the United States a world leader in higher education attainment by 2020. I urge the Senate to pass that critical legislation. For the same reasons that underlie the broad AGI initiative, community colleges should play a central role in the WIA system as well. Community colleges are the primary "on ramp" for the majority of low-wage and first-generation college goers in America. Community colleges are America's public asset in moving low-skill workers into higher-paying careers. Whether it be educating low-skilled adults and those with limited English proficiency and transitioning them to post-secondary education, developing and offering cutting-edge occupational programs, or working directly with businesses to help train their workers, community colleges are a natural hub of the workforce development system. But too often, community colleges are regarded as mere vendors in a system where they should be looked upon and behave as true partners.

Some States have positioned community colleges strategically as the hub of their workforce development system. For example, in my home State of Virginia, the Governor asked the community college system to administer the WIA program and to serve as staff to the State workforce investment board. The reasoning behind this move was simple: in an era in which high school is no longer the finish line, State and Federal programs should utilize and support the public asset that anchors workforce development at the post-secondary education level—the community college. On a national level, however, WIA is essentially agnostic as to training providers. Prioritizing the role of community colleges is key to strengthening the system overall. Community colleges are the closest thing this country has to a national network of ubiquitous, low-cost and high-quality training providers, and the WIA legislation should reflect that. Community colleges are a national asset that WIA is not leveraging to its fullest.

One such community college is Northern Virginia Community College. NOVA has developed new ways that community colleges and community-based non-profit job training programs can work together to help low-income Americans secure higher paying jobs and long-term career advancement by rapidly progressing toward a post-secondary credential. I would like to describe three such partnerships between NOVA and community-based organizations to help illustrate the points I want to make regarding WIA reauthorization.

TRAINING FUTURES

One of these is a program that integrates the training provided by a community-based organization with NOVA's post-secondary certificate program in office administration. For the past 6 years, NOVA has teamed with Northern Virginia Family Service (NVFS), a community-based 501(c)3 non-profit organization that assists low-income families with challenges that range from health and housing issues to economic concerns and traumatic crises. NVFS has a training program named Training Futures (TF) that targets underemployed and unemployed Northern Virginia family breadwinners. Three-fourths of the trainees are immigrants. Most are stuck in dead-end retail, service and manual labor jobs paying an average wage of $10.00 an hour with no benefits. Two-thirds are trying to raise families with an average annual income of $20,000. Many of these family breadwinners wake up every day knowing they may be just one missed paycheck from receiving an eviction notice. Without upgrading their skills for new jobs, these working poor can remain stuck for years living on the edge of homelessness. And, without a post-secondary credential, their chances of upward mobility are slim to none.

Training Futures delivers a 24-week comprehensive training and internship program targeted at entry-level health care office administration jobs. Because of its partnership with NOVA, TF graduates leave the program with marketable skills *and* a jump start toward a college degree with 17 college credits. Through this community college-nonprofit workforce development partnership, over 500 low-income trainees at Training Futures have earned college credits to help them launch and advance new careers. Earning college credits gives TF graduates an edge in competing for scores of job openings in northern Virginia that list "some college preferred" on job ads. Despite the recession and decline in hiring, Training Futures' job placement outcomes have remained in the 80 percent range.

According to a recent third-party survey, one-third of TF's graduates have continued working toward an associate degree at NOVA after graduating from the program. Were it not for the special collaboration between NOVA and Training Futures, it is likely that most program completers would have little prospect of achieving a post-secondary credential or career mobility. By creating an "on ramp" to college, NOVA and TF have created the pathway for continuing professional development that helps graduates accelerate their career advancement and job security, with two-thirds of graduates reporting promotions. It also contributes to nearly doubling of graduates' earnings to over $35,000 at the time of the graduate survey. In addition to graduates' wage increases, the survey also documented an 82 percent increase in home ownership, doubling of the proportion of trainees receiving employment benefits such as health care insurance, and doubling of average family savings.

YEAR UP

Year Up is another example of a community-based non-profit that teams with NOVA in the Washington, DC metro area. It offers a 1-year, intensive training program, providing a combination of technical and professional skills in information technology, an educational stipend and corporate internships. Working with NOVA, the program offers a semester's worth of college credit to those completing the program. Year Up students are young adults between the ages of 18 and 24 who know they can do better than remaining in minimum-wage jobs. Some are single parents. But with only a high school education, they lack the skills, experience, and credentials to launch themselves onto a career track. They see Year Up as their launching pad for both an IT career and a start in college, especially now that graduates receive college credit from Northern Virginia Community College. Within 4 months of graduation, nearly 80 percent of Year Up completers are employed with average earnings of over $35,000 a year. Year Up currently serves more than 1,600 students a year at sites in Atlanta, Boston, Providence, New York City, San Francisco, and Washington, DC.

GOODWILL INDUSTRIES INTERNATIONAL

A third example of community college-CBO partnership illustrates the potential power that a collaborative relationship between America's community colleges and community-based nonprofits could have if scaled nationally. Last November, national leaders from Goodwill Industries International, the Nation's largest non-profit job training provider, teamed with NOVA and a group of America's community colleges to chart a national strategy to help thousands of low-income Americans nationwide achieve extraordinary job and college attainment results. The vision is to create a national workforce development strategy between the Nation's community colleges and Goodwill Industries International, to provide skills training to low-income individuals *and* to create an explicit pathway toward a post-secondary credential and a family-sustaining wage with healthcare and retirement benefits. Such a partnership between America's 1,200 community colleges and Goodwill Industries offices nationally that serve 1.5 million low-income and disabled individuals annually offers an unprecedented opportunity for our country to help low-income Americans achieve self sufficiency and build a more competitive economy.

THE CURRENT WIA ENVIRONMENT

In northern Virginia, NOVA and the Northern Virginia Workforce Investment Board have a strong history of collaboration, focusing on:
• targeted industry and occupational training, particularly in nursing and allied health worker training and teaming through a WIA Community-Based Job Training Grant;
• job placement within high impact employers and industries. In Northern Virginia, NOVA has consistently been the largest training provider of WIA training programs in the region;
• collaborative service strategies, such as workforce board-administered career centers on NOVA campuses or NOVA employer outreach teams based at Northern Virginia Workforce Board's Comprehensive Workforce Centers; and
• win-win efforts on behalf of both workers and the region's businesses. In 2009, the Northern Virginia Workforce Board funded an economic feasibility study to develop a new workforce development center on one of NOVA's campuses. That study will be the basis by which NOVA will seek additional State funding to build this center.

But, even with the strong relationship with the northern Virginia WIB, NOVA's CBO partnerships all face significant challenges in qualifying for or working with WIA funding due to WIA's current emphasis:
• Funding tends to favor short-term skills training and immediate employment rather than supporting longer-term career development and transitions toward achieving a post-secondary credential;
• Establishing trainee/student eligibility is a cumbersome and difficult process, leading many community colleges and CBOs to direct their efforts to other than WIA-supported training;
• Community colleges tend to be regarded as simply another training provider rather than a critical hub of the public workforce development system;
• There are few incentives to recognize or reward collaboration, innovation, or leveraging resources between key players within the workforce development system;
• Funding criteria emphasize direct training services rather than critical capacity building that incentivizes effective programs to achieve scale and sustainability.

RECOMMENDATIONS OFFERED FOR CONSIDERATION IN WIA REAUTHORIZATION

1. Strengthen Pathways to Post-Secondary Credential Attainment

The Nation's economy requires that an unprecedented increase in the percentage of the population who achieve market-valued post-secondary credentials. Achieving this goal will require a multi-faceted effort on the parts of institutions, States and the Federal Government. This effort will only succeed if we are effective in reaching out to populations that are currently underrepresented in post-secondary education, such as those participants in CBO training programs, and design training pathways at the post-secondary level that lead to high-wage employment. In WIA reauthorization, Congress has a significant opportunity to assist this effort by providing support for increased linkages between community-based organizations that do workforce training and post-secondary education institutions such as community colleges. The CBO-to-postsecondary "pipeline" is vital to achieving the post-secondary credential achievement rates that are required to maintain our Nation's economic competitiveness.

To improve the functioning of the CBO-to-postsecondary pipeline, the following features are recommended:

• Add "transition to post-secondary education and training" to the purposes of the act and the definition of adult education, and clarify throughout the act that transition programs can and should be funded with WIA funds.

• Include a measure of the total number of people served by the workforce development system who make the transition to post-secondary education and training in the performance accountability system.

• Require eligible agencies to consider, when deciding on local grants and contracts, whether grantees offer explicit provisions for post-secondary transition.

• Prioritize youth programs that have strong connections to post-secondary education.

2. Encourage Collaboration & Innovation Between Key Workforce Development Stake Holders

Congress should think broadly about the most effective ways to administer WIA funds at the regional and local level, to ensure the proper mix between assisting participant access to training and the development of training capacity:

• Authorize sector initiatives. Sector initiatives bring together training providers, businesses, WIBs, economic development and other key partners to develop training programs and train workers and provide other services to help important local business sectors thrive. These initiatives are a particularly effective way of ensuring that workers are receiving training for available, good jobs. WIA should provide State and local areas with ample latitude to design such initiatives that best suit their needs. Community colleges should be regarded as key partners in any such program that receives WIA support. The Community-Based Job Training Grant program provides a model that should be used when designing sector initiatives within the WIA formula programs.

• Establish incentive grants to reward innovative and effective programs. Incentive grants should reward more than just meeting a numerical benchmark. They should spur the innovative, effective and coordinated approaches devised at the State and local levels that other areas should emulate. Effective utilization of community colleges—community-based partnerships should be one of the considerations in deciding grant recipients.

• Help successful programs scale so they can increase their impact and be sustainable.

• Promote and ensure an efficient and effective coordination of investments and services across a wide range of programs, providers, and systems, particularly those such as WIA's own adult, dislocated, and youth funding, Wagner-Peyser Employment Services, Trade Adjustment Assistance, Pell grants for Unemployment Insurance claimants, and Re-employment Eligibility Assessment.

• Strengthen ties to such programs as Carl Perkins, TANF, ABE, Food Stamps Training programs, and other programs that seek to provide skills development and employment assistance to our Nation's workers. Congress should insist that these programs be administered consistently at the One-Stop Employment Centers, rather than the multiple other methods of service delivery. This one action will move the system towards greater integration, on behalf of the job seeker.

3. Provide More Support for the Expansion of Training Capacity

Community colleges place top priority on efforts to help students access post-secondary education and training. However, many community colleges are straining to serve all the students who are enrolling. In economic downturns such as the one we are now experiencing, double-digit percentage increases in enrollment from one year to the next are the norm. According to a recent survey by the American Association of Community Colleges (AACC), community college enrollments have increased by 16.9 percent in the last 2 years. These enrollment increases are often not covered by State appropriations, so colleges are forced to raise tuition (if they have that authority), cut expenses to the bone, or turn students away from their programs. Often, it will be a combination of all three. The average community college derives approximately 20 percent of its revenue through tuition and fees, which gives some idea of the percentage of the college's actual program costs that are covered by individual training accounts.

WIA should provide more direct support for additional training capacity at community colleges. Without a Federal priority on developing this capacity, WIA participants will continue to face less effective, more expensive options if they wish to immediately access training. Businesses will struggle to find candidates with the skills that they need for available jobs.

Congress can take some simple, but meaningful, steps in this direction under the current WIA structure:

• Authorize the Community-Based Job Training Grants (CBJTGs), which were created in 2004 in response to this capacity crunch. The CBJTGs are a sector initiative that is funded and is working. The program should be authorized as it was originally envisioned, namely a national competitive grant program that awards grants to community colleges, working in partnership with local WIBs, businesses and other key stakeholders to expand training capacity at the college and train workers for high-demand occupations. Unfortunately, the Administration has proposed the elimination of this program in its fiscal year 2011 budget. The support this program offers is crucial, and it would be a mistake to eliminate it. As I mentioned earlier, it should also be a model for incorporating sector strategies into the WIA formula programs.

• Give local workforce boards greater flexibility to utilize training contracts, especially with low-tuition training providers such as community colleges. This approach was taken in the American Recovery and Reinvestment Act because Congress recognized it as a way to expeditiously and effectively train workers and stimulate the economy. It should be made a permanent part of WIA.

CONCLUSION

America's community-based non-profit organizations have several distinctive strengths often not found in American higher education. CBO's are particularly successful in reaching low-income populations who are not in school. Many of these participants need entry-level job skills, additional support services in order to complete job training programs, and quick job placement results that are often not available from colleges. America's 1,400 non-profit CBO workforce development providers serve several million adults annually. Their entry-level job training programs represent a great beginning, but typically they are not sufficient to move low-skill workers into sustainable careers with livable wages and benefits. For that to happen, some form of post-secondary credential is needed. America's 1,177 community colleges can do the job of linking CBO job training with college opportunity. College credentials are America's surest ticket to long-term success. Americans with associate degrees earn 29 percent more than high school graduates, and are 30 percent less likely to be unemployed.

CBO's and community colleges offer complementary assets. Community colleges and community-based organizations already have mission alignment to train moderate-income young adults and low-wage workers. CBO's excel at job skills training, job placement, and specialized support services for immediate job and wage-gain results. Community colleges provide low-cost college education opportunities, access to Federal financial aid (Pell grants) and college credentials for long-term career advancement.

Together, the Nation's community colleges and community-based organizations can form key components of a comprehensive workforce development system operating to the benefit of workers, the unemployed and America's businesses, *IF* they join their extraordinary job training and educational outcomes together. What is needed is a workforce system that incentivizes them to work as one.

Thank you, Mr. Chairman and members of the committee for this opportunity to speak with you today.

Senator CASEY. Thank you very much.

I am going to, for purposes of moving our hearing along, postpone my questioning. I will turn first to our Ranking Member, Senator Enzi, and then go to Senator Brown. I know Senator Brown has to leave, and we will try to be as flexible as we can with other members as well.

Senator Enzi.

Senator ENZI. Thank you, Mr. Chairman.

I have to do some work on healthcare, too. This is equally important to healthcare. I want you to know that it bears that kind of importance for me. We have been working on it for years, and it is time to get it done.

I appreciate the comments of everybody. They have been excellent. It doesn't matter who we have testifying, even with Governors and veterans and others that we have had testify in past hearings, the message is pretty much all the same. And that is we really need to do something in this area, that we need to get rid of the silos, build in some flexibility, and there needs to be increased funding.

Now, I believe that if we ever get this reauthorized, there will be more funding. Right now, we are not using all of the funds because of the silos, and that is a counter argument to provide more funding. I think we can make the changes.

I will begin with Mr. Stalknecht. Last week, I was in Wyoming. I went to an organization that is now nationwide. They train mechanics for diesel trucks and cars and do what you were talking about. It is called WyoTech. I agree that we need to change the culture, and we need to have the on-the-job training. I am committed to a workforce system that job seekers and employers can use.

How can we continue to engage business to be a part of the decisions related to skill training, to education, and workforce development? What types of roles does business find most meaningful?

Mr. STALKNECHT. Thank you, Senator.

Small businesses and the ones I represent, as I indicated before, average about $1 million revenue, less than 10 employees. Obviously, we have some that are much larger. It is time constraints that they have as business owners, trying to operate a small business and also working with some of the WIA boards around the country.

Their frustration is the bureaucracy that is there and the inertia that happens at some of these workforce development boards, where they spend a lot of time, and they just don't have the time to give. They sort of lose their interest in that.

If there is some way that they can streamline the processes at these workforce development boards, where it would be more objective to the effort rather than just continually having meetings and meetings and requiring small businesses to attend. They just don't have the time. There has to be some flexibility, as we heard from my colleagues here today, in some of these activities, but more importantly, recognizing the constraints on the small businesses. They want to help, but they just don't have the time in many cases.

Senator ENZI. In some of the hearings I have held, the number of small businesses has been small—they said, "How come that is all that showed up?" I said, "Well, if they had enough people to come to a meeting that they didn't think was worthwhile, they would fire them."

[Laughter.]

Mr. Templin, as a former small business owner, I believe that it is important to encourage entrepreneurship in communities, and that is why I host an inventors conference each year in Wyoming, which opens the door to businesses to help make ideas a reality. Based on your experience, how can community programs that train entrepreneurs impact the workforce development system, and what, if anything, could reauthorization include to encourage more entrepreneurship in the communities?

Mr. TEMPLIN. That is an excellent question. Community colleges are just at the early stages of making linkages between entrepreneurs and formal training, and we have significant models of success. Unfortunately, the stovepipes that we have between WIA training and higher education training tend to have different rules and different metrics that create different incentives.

Consequently, it is the unusual community college that works with the workforce investment board around the area of entrepreneurship. More likely, they are going to develop a relationship with a community-based nonprofit that is already serving minority, low income, or immigrant populations and encourage those students to enter their continuing education or credit courses without a connection to WIA.

It is a missing opportunity for us to work across boundaries and to integrate the region's resources to the benefit of our people.

Senator ENZI. Thank you. My time is almost up.

I have questions for all of you, and I appreciate you volunteering to be on this panel. I hope that you will answer some questions in writing because we can usually get into a little bit more detail. It is really the detail that helps us on this.

I would appreciate that, and I will yield back the rest of my time.

Senator CASEY. Thank you, Senator Enzi.

Senator Brown.

STATEMENT OF SENATOR BROWN

Senator BROWN. Thank you very much, Mr. Chair. Thanks for going a bit out of order. I appreciate that.

Ms. Feldman, I would like to ask you about sectors and the importance that you have attached to it and the community colleges, Dr. Templin, the importance that you have attached to it. Our SECTORS Act, our legislation is basically founded on, as Senator Enzi suggested, that it is from the bottom up. That you work with local businesses, local labor unions, local workforce investment boards, and local schools, universities, especially community colleges. My State has a terrific network of them, as many other States do.

One example in Ohio of where this has worked. In Fremont, Ohio, a city not too far from Lake Erie, they have had a marine trade sector partnership. It is in northwest Ohio. Most of the boats registered in Lake Erie, some 400,000, are not far or are in the northwest part of the State between Cleveland and Toledo.

There is a demand for trained skilled labor in the marine trade industry, but they simply don't have enough people in those that are skilled to do the kind of maintenance and other things for these 400,000 boats that are registered there.

Talk to me about, and you think about—I think any one of us could take a tour of our States and point out, for instance, I would say in Toledo, Toledo has more solar energy manufacturing jobs than any city in the country. That would be something that local businesses and community college would want to concentrate on. Or you could go to Philadelphia. You could go different places and do the same around the country.

A couple of questions. What, in your mind, Ms. Feldman, are the key elements of effective sectors partnerships? Also, how do existing WIA programs help or hinder the development of more robust sector partnerships? If you could speak generally and as specific as you can about both of those?

Ms. FELDMAN. OK. I think what makes sector partnerships work, first of all, is you have to have an innovative leader to the partnership. That can vary from community to community. In some cases, it might be a community college. In other cases, it might be a WIB or it might be a labor-management partnership.

I think there has to be flexibility in letting that bubble up out of the community or the region that is involved because that workforce intermediary has to be respected to bring those partners around the table, multiple partners. To really initiate workforce programs that are not just run of the mill, but involve a lot of innovation, which requires that people break down the barriers between their various organizations and work together to create the kind of innovative opportunities that are possible.

The other piece is it has to be results-oriented, in my opinion. The work of that sector needs to really look at data, carefully analyze the labor market data, and then decide on a strategy driven by that data that is going to get results for that industry. That employer voice is really important. The labor voice is really important in determining that. All voices need to be heard at that table.

I think I could give you some examples. In Philadelphia, for example, we were able to actually use an H–1B grant, as opposed to a WIA grant, to train 1,700 nurses that met the nursing needs across numerous employers. Forty-five schools were involved in this partnership at the community college level, at the hospital level, schools of nursing, as well as at the university level.

In order to make that happen, we had to have the support of the businesses because they provided a lot of in-kind and cash match to it. We had to have the support of the WIA system to embrace it and support it. Most importantly, I think we needed a leader, and that came in the form of our labor-management partnership that had the vision that this was possible.

Senator BROWN. Let me interrupt you for a second.

Ms. FELDMAN. Yes.

Senator BROWN. What you just said about a leader, and what you said earlier, that it is important that someone rise to the occasion on this. If we integrate this SECTORS Act into our reauthorization, as most people, I think, in both parties want to see us do something along those lines as a central part of workforce investment, can we assume that in community after community, creating it this way will make the leader rise to the top? Is there a way of guaranteeing that?

I mean, we don't obviously mandate it needs to be in this case a community college, this place a business leader, this time a union leader, this time a workforce investment board person. I mean, how do we build this so it produces one or two or three people that are really going to pick it up like that?

Ms. FELDMAN. I think this is where the legislation really needs to support flexibility and really needs to support the opportunity for communities to come forward and say here is this track record.

We already have capacity. We don't have to start from scratch. As opposed to initiatives which constantly ask us to form new partnerships and prove something when it is already existing. Are you following me?

The WIA legislation has not been particularly supportive of sector initiatives. The only reason we have been able to do it successfully in Philadelphia is because of the industry partnership model that was established at the State and also our training fund, our Taft-Hartley fund, which created this industry partnership in 1974. We have 49 employers that pay 1.5 percent of gross payroll into the Taft-Hartley fund.

We all sit around the same table. We all have common interests to resolve the problems that face us as an industry.

Senator BROWN. OK. Thank you very much.

Thanks, Mr. Chairman.

[The prepared statement of Senator Brown follows:]

PREPARED STATEMENT OF SENATOR BROWN

Thank you, Chairman Harkin and Senator Enzi for calling this hearing. And thank you to the witnesses for joining us this morning.

The reauthorization of the Workforce Investment Act should be a central plank in our jobs recovery strategy.

At this point last year, we were hemorrhaging jobs at a rate of more than 600,000 per month. Today, we have stopped the bleeding but economists tell us that the job market will not fully recover for several years.

According to the Bureau of Labor Statistics, since the start of the recession, 5 million people have joined the ranks of the long-term unemployed. We now have 6.3 million workers who have been without jobs for 27 weeks or more compared to 1.3 million at the start of the recession. In Ohio, 641,000 people are unemployed—an increase of 196,000 from last year.

Even during these very tough times in the job market, I hear from employers who are struggling to find workers with the skills that are needed to grow their businesses. Some of these are in the technology, health, and energy sectors. There has been a mismatch between our education and job training programs and the emerging sectors in our economy.

That is why I introduced the Strengthening Employment Clusters to Organize Regional Success Act—also known as the SECTORS Act to align our education, job training, and economic development with key industry sectors to strengthen regional economies. We know that sectoral strategies work, yet our stove-piped workforce systems do not facilitate them.

Consider the results of the marine trades sector to partnership in Fremont, OH. In and around the rural communities that surround Lake Erie, marine trade occupations are difficult to recruit and maintain a high level of expertise. But each year, there are more than 400,000 boats registered in Ohio, with most in northwest Ohio. So, there is a demand for trained skilled labor in the marine trades industry. Labor and community colleges, along with the WIBs, have teamed up with employers to develop the "Skills for Life" Marine Trades Training Initiative.

This is just one example in my State, but there are dozens more in Iowa, Wyoming, Washington, and Georgia.

We cannot return to sustainable job and wage growth without modernizing our workforce investment system. I am eager to hear the witnesses' recommendations on how we can break down the silos in the current system and create the conditions for advancement for our workers and for our economy.

Thank you.

Senator CASEY. Senator Reed.

Senator REED. I yield to Senator Franken.

STATEMENT OF SENATOR FRANKEN

Senator FRANKEN. Thank you, Senator.

I guess I will go to Mr. Stalknecht. You represent small businesses, right, that do air conditioning, and you basically use WIA and workforce investment boards as a source of the people you represent, source of getting good workers, right?

Mr. STALKNECHT. Senator, that is one avenue we use. I don't know specifically to the extent of how widespread it is in our industry. We do know that, in fact, we had some information on that, and I can provide it to you a little bit later on, as to the placements from the WIA into the HVAC industry. I don't have that right at my fingertips.

What we found most successful in our industry is two things. One is when we developed our own apprenticeship programs that were funded by the local contractor in conjunction with, for example, Montgomery Community College.

Then we also found that many companies, the ones who are a little bit bigger of scale, had the ability to create their own apprenticeship program. We had one very successful one, Service Legends in Des Moines, IA, for example. They created their own program, and they get, from what I understand, over 100 applicants a month just to go into that program.

The question we have is, is when we have these companies that can afford to have apprenticeship programs and we have then an interest in the community, there is a disconnect where we don't get them from the high school feeder system into the industry. That is really our frustration because what we found in our experiences in dealing with guidance counselors around the country, they just are not proficient in understanding the opportunities in the skilled trades.

Senator FRANKEN. They can go to a board, a workforce investment board and get referrals?

Mr. STALKNECHT. That is correct. We have to back that up a little bit and get some information into the high school guidance counselors, into the high school systems about skilled trades. Not just for our industry, but you have the electrical trades. You have the plumbing trades. You have the construction trades, the whole gamut of a skilled workforce base.

Senator FRANKEN. Is it fair to say, and I will ask this of everyone, that one of the jobs of WIA is to be sort of a one-stop shopping place for both people who need jobs and local people who need employees? Anybody?

Mr. CARNEVALE. Well, there is a distinction. That is, there are the U.S. employment services, which are a separate institution pretty much entirely, that are separated from the WIA One-Stops. The employment services are where we keep information on what the—that is where you apply if you are looking for a job.

The opportunity loss there, I think, because it is our labor exchange, is that people—I think we are talking 30 million or so in this recession—have applied for unemployment insurance, and nobody ever gave them any conversation, counseling, and the information they might need to figure out what they are going to do next.

The One-Stops have essentially been an attempt to do that, but they have become very separated from the core institution where the data is, which is in the employment where the people come and where the data is. For instance, if you wanted to know whether we should fund this industry partnership or not, first thing I would want to know is are there going to be any jobs there based on retirement of current workers and on projected growth?

You would have to figure that out from the trends. If someone started a brand-new industry, you wouldn't have much to say about it. I am not sure you would want to start brand-new industries with public money, frankly. I think you would want some kind of track record.

If you wanted to know what the wages are, the employment service knows. They track the wages of all Americans on a quarterly basis, and they can tell you which occupations pay and which don't. In many respects, we separated our WIA system from the mother ship over the last quite a few years.

Senator FRANKEN. You are saying we should get more coordination?

Mr. CARNEVALE. I am saying in the end that I think reorganizing institutions tends to be a waste of time. I think we ought to do this with information. That is, we ought to know where the jobs are going to be, what they are going to pay. We ought to know the programs we put people into. If we attach the programs to the wage records that are kept by the employment service, we can know exactly how much they made and if they were employed as a result of the program.

I would coordinate these institutions with information systems and counseling, not by reorganizing the institutions themselves.

Senator FRANKEN. OK. I am out of my time. Mr. Chairman, may I ask Mr. Templin one question?

Senator CASEY. You may.

Senator FRANKEN. Thank you.

I have heard concerns from representatives of both business and labor organizations in Minnesota about training offerings in their community, and in some areas, community college programs vital to local businesses have been cut, and in others, community college programs have been created that appear to duplicate existing training programs provided by labor organizations. For example, the IBEW in Rochester, MN, is training their workers in working on wind energy, and at the same time, some of the community colleges are doing the same. The jobs just aren't there.

Has this been a problem that you have run into, and can you suggest strategies for ensuring better coordination between training programs?

Mr. TEMPLIN. I have seen some duplication, but not what I would call unnecessary duplication. In other words, I have seen multiple providers in a particular space where the demand for jobs really is there.

In cases where demand is projected, but not currently there, I would hope that WIA would encourage this collaboration across lines so that the union and the community college could develop appropriate divisions of labor. A union will not be able very easily to grant a portable credential that you can stack toward a bachelor's degree if an individual experiences success and wants to go on.

Similarly, a community college probably cannot create the kind of workplace training that a union can create. We need incentives that cause these institutions to work together for greater efficiency and effectiveness and hold them accountable for it.

Senator FRANKEN. Thank you. Thank you very much.

Thank you, Mr. Chairman.

Senator CASEY. Thank you, Senator Franken.

Senator Reed.

STATEMENT OF SENATOR REED

Senator REED. Thank you very much, Mr. Chairman.

Thank you for your excellent testimony.

Let me address a question to you individually and to the whole panel, which reflects some of the comments that were raised in Senator Franken's question. What is the general ability and adequacy of aligning training programs with jobs, which, we hope, is going to be part of the reauthorization? How do we make sure that we are responding to the jobs of the immediate present and the near future and not training the proverbial rope-maker or something like that?

Mr. Carnevale, do you have any thoughts? Just quickly your comments, and we will go down the line.

Mr. CARNEVALE. Yes. To be sort of mechanical about it, I would use employer-based wage records, which are reported quarterly, tie those to transcript curriculums wherever they come from, proprietary schools or community colleges, 4-year, unions, or whatever. Thereby, I would know whether or not somebody got a job, how many hours they worked, and how much they made as a result of completing the program.

Then I would use that same information as counseling information for the workers themselves. The information is not useful to the workers, I think, unless there is some counseling as a piece to it.

We do not do a very good job at all of connecting our programs to current or prospective labor demand. We largely operate on the basis of whatever somebody wrote in the U.S. News and World Report this week.

Green jobs is a case in point. Between now and 2018, we will probably have about 3 million green jobs, probably 5 million or 6 million openings given retirements. That is out of 162 million jobs.

There is a certain sort of style factor that goes decade by decade with jobs. We do have the data. That is what is pretty stunning about all this.

Senator REED. Thank you.

Mr. Carbone.

Mr. CARBONE. Yes, this is, I think, part of a leadership role on a regional level for workforce investment boards. We are supposed to be a voice. We are supposed to be a convener. Our job is to collect the data, interpret it, and communicate it.

It seems to me that it brings it down to that local delivery level again. That if it is functioning as it is prescribed under the Workforce Investment Act, all the partners are getting all the information, and it is the same information, and there is leadership at the top of the system to ensure that all the partners are cooperating. Which means that the trainers are getting programs ready that are consistent with economic trends, that everybody is not trying to do the exact same thing.

We are taking the best of what the community colleges can do or training from the labor side or other groups. It is being done in a way in which there is leadership to it.

I think the act clearly gives that responsibility at the local level to workforce investment boards. I think what is incumbent upon this committee as you consider the reauthorization is to put the tools in the act to make sure all workforce boards do what workforce boards are supposed to do.

Senator REED. Mr. Stalknecht.

Mr. STALKNECHT. Yes. My recommendation would be to look at some of the private sector apprenticeship programs that are ongoing right now, that are very successful. As the one illustrated that I talked about before with the Washington, DC area capital, they receive, to the best of my knowledge, very little or no Government funding.

The problem we have is trying to expand those successful models around the country, which can work. We know they can. The problem with supporting a private sector type of apprenticeship program, it could be tied in very easily to some of the workforce boards, but there are models out there in various private sector industries that do work, and we need to find out why they work, why they are successful.

They are jobs. They are the energy-related jobs that are out there. We just need to find mechanisms to expand them throughout the country for the workforce that we need of the future.

Senator REED. Before I recognize Ms. Feldman, would it be helpful to require or as part of the Federal contracting process, at least give credit for apprenticeship programs as an incentive to move the process along? Has that been considered?

Mr. STALKNECHT. We have a program in the National Capital Chapter that works with Montgomery Community College. As I indicated before, there is about 640 classroom hours and 8,000 on-the-job hours. There is an accreditation program that goes along with recognition of the on-the-job training.

Senator REED. My thought would be if, for example, one of the factors in a contract for a radar system was a plus for a valid apprenticeship program in the applicant, would that be helpful, in your view?

Mr. STALKNECHT. Well, it would be something to think about, and I would assume it would be very helpful. Recognizing that in the HVAC industry, we are a microcosm of business in general, where probably about 90 percent of the businesses in the industry are nonunion. So they are smaller companies. What we have is very, very good union apprenticeship programs, but where we need help and support is to represent those 90 percent of businesses that are not union and don't have the wherewithal to put together an apprenticeship program.

You take the residential side. Residential are the technicians or the businesses that serve your home and everybody in this room. Probably 99 percent of those companies are nonunion. And what we need to find is the workforce to help that and programs that would help the nonunion contractors with apprenticeship programs.

Senator REED. Ms. Feldman, would you like to respond to your comrades' comments, or respond to the issue of aligning supply and demand?

Ms. FELDMAN. I would like to do both. In terms of, first, the aligning jobs, I think that is where the sector approach that Senator Brown was talking about is really important. Because when you get employers and labor and others around the table from the same sector—health and life sciences, for example—they know what is going on on the ground, and they know where the jobs are going. That kind of strategic thinking, as part of that sector approach, is really important.

In Pennsylvania, we established the Pennsylvania Center for Healthcare, which is a statewide sector for the healthcare industry. We have done incredible data work to identify where the jobs are and where they are going through 2016, and it has driven then all the decisions we are making in the State through the WIB level and through our partnership. So I think that sector approach is really important.

In terms of apprenticeships, we have done some in our union. Not as much as the construction trades, but I think that there are models certainly on the labor side that are really beneficial to linking apprenticeship to college credits and to the credentials that they need so that it is more of a portable credential that is recognized across the industry.

We have become a big fan of giving credit for technical training. I think that kind of model brings in the community college piece, the labor piece, the employer piece. Once you have a model like that, it can be replicated, and I think that is really important.

Senator REED. Thank you.

Mr. Templin.

Mr. TEMPLIN. My advice would be that taking pieces of what have been said, that the watch word isn't a cookie cutter approach, but that the WIB must be given flexibility. In a sector strategy, the WIB might not be the appropriate organization to lead the sector activity, but it could be very important to convening it and supporting it.

With regard to data, having data available for the sector—meaning the employers, labor, and the training providers—to talk with one another is incredibly important to connect jobs, training with jobs. Just looking at the data through the WIB without that conversation is not necessarily valuable. Let me give you a case in point.

Right now, if you talk to at least hospitals in this region, healthcare systems in this region, they will tell you that they are not hiring many RNs. That doesn't mean that there is not a shortage. It takes years to develop that talent.

If we crank down the system so that there aren't people in the pipeline, without a conversation and go only by the data, you will be seriously misled. It only works when industry is involved not as a spectator, but as a business proposition, knowing that it is vital to their future and that they are giving something, not just taking something, but they are contributing something.

And that training organizations are held accountable not just for completing programs, but placing graduates in real jobs. That is what the WIB can do as a facilitator in a process. It doesn't have to always be the actor in a sector strategy. It often doesn't have the expertise, but it does have a framework that if it is given flexibility can help this country a great deal.

Senator REED. Thank you very much.

Thank you, Mr. Chairman.

Senator CASEY. Thank you, Senator Reed.

I want to thank our witnesses for your testimony. I have a number of questions. Let me just start by way of a comment.

I have often said—and it might be somewhat of an exaggeration, but I think it is within the ballpark of what is out there in the real world—that if you had to boil down to two words what is the biggest economic challenge the Commonwealth of Pennsylvania faces, and I think it is true across the country, you could probably boil it down to those two words meaning "workforce development."

Obviously, when you talk about this subject and you say flatly that that is one of, if not the central challenge of our economy going forward, there is a lot under that umbrella.

Obviously, when you talk about if you are going to have a workforce development or a skills strategy so that we can compete in the world economy, that means that a child gets healthcare, nutrition, and early learning. It means that we have good primary and secondary education. It means that we have the whole range of higher education opportunities. It means that we have great training programs in place.

It is easy to say it in two words, but it does imply, I think, having a lot of pillars to undergird that goal. I know that in Pennsylvania—and Ms. Feldman referred to a couple of examples. I know that in Pennsylvania, we have made great strides not only with the implementation of the act and making improvements, but she just mentioned, for example, the regional partnerships.

We have talked a lot about partnerships today, and I am looking at a—I won't obviously read all this. It is a publication by the State industry partnerships in Pennsylvania. Here on page 7, you have the Northeastern Pennsylvania Regional Healthcare Industry Partnership, as well as the South Central Pennsylvania Healthcare Partnership.

46

It is happening, I know, not only in Pennsylvania, but in other States. We can further develop that.

One additional comment about what I have seen in Pennsylvania, especially when I was in State government for a decade, the remarkable story of community colleges. We have 14 in Pennsylvania. We could probably use a few more.

Maybe one of the most unheralded, underrated, underestimated, underappreciated education sectors that I can think of or, for that matter, beyond education. Tremendous strides we have made because of the impact of our community colleges.

Let me get to a question. But before I do, I do want to recognize someone over the right shoulder of Ms. Feldman, Henry Nicholas, a distinguished labor leader with tremendous experience, real experience in training people for the jobs of the future in healthcare. Henry, we are grateful you are here. Next time we have one of these, we will add a chair and you can come up and provide testimony.

Your work has been your testimony for a lot of years. We are grateful for your leadership.

I wanted to get back to some of the questions we have moved through before, and I want to try as best we can, and I won't direct these in every instance to an individual witness but have people jump in when you want to. Two broad questions—one about flexibility and the other about this, it has been expressed in different ways, but something that I have heard over the years when I have been on the road, so to speak, listening to the complaints, concerns, or criticisms about our workforce development system and, in particular, the act.

Some of this is a little dated because I think we have made progress on it. Just this disconnect between the needs of employers and what or who is coming through the pipeline, that basic disconnect.

I know, Ms. Feldman, I will start with you, but I want to involve everyone in this. On I think it is the second page of your testimony, you say, "Employers in the region lack a strong talent pipeline to fill critical jobs." Now I have heard this over the years in a lot of different contexts. Not just they lack enough of a pipeline of a specific skill. That is one thing I have heard.

I have also heard that sometimes there is a broader base and a sometimes lower, but important skill level. If someone is hired to work in an office as something as basic and fundamental as a receptionist, they don't know sometimes how to answer a telephone. They don't know how to interact with people. They don't have some basic literacy skills. Then it goes above that to higher and much more precise skill levels.

I wanted to have you comment on that in the context of Philadelphia and Pennsylvania. Then I want to have others weigh in as well.

Ms. FELDMAN. I really thank you for that opportunity because one of the things we haven't talked about today is the importance of literacy, and what we are finding in Philadelphia is that—and there is a great publication called Tale of Two Cities put out by our Philadelphia WIB.

Senator CASEY. I have it here, actually.

Ms. FELDMAN. There you go. That 50 percent——

Senator CASEY. I am sorry. This is called Help Wanted. But it is similar.

Ms. FELDMAN. OK, same. Second edition. Fifty percent of our citizens in Philadelphia do not have the literacy skills needed, and that includes working people. We seem to focus, you know, on the needs of the K through 12 system. We have adults who are working and not working who don't have the literacy skills to serve as that talent pipeline for employers.

The statistics we came up with in Philadelphia was that 30 percent of the jobs require some kind of higher level—not even higher level, but some real literacy skill. We have 50 percent of our population trying to squeeze into 30 percent of the jobs. That is a real problem.

What happens in the WIA system is we don't have the funds, and sometimes it is expensive. We don't have the funds to really work with that—with half of our population who are ready, willing, and able to get the skills they need to move into real jobs in the healthcare system. With the budget cuts at the State, part of our literacy money comes from the Feds, part comes from the State— 30 percent cut in the State budget.

I don't see literacy being addressed in the WIA Act as something——

Senator CASEY. I was going to ask you that.

Ms. FELDMAN. As something that can be used to really impact this pipeline. The employers need the talent pool, and the workers need the jobs. But without that piece that is missing, how are we going to get there? I mean, there are so many great models, including ones that we have developed, but we don't have the funding for it.

It really is an enigma to me why we can't understand that our economy is being held hostage by the lack of literacy skills of huge chunks in our population.

Senator CASEY. I want to involve others. In addition to literacy, just on this question of the disconnect because business leaders have said to me over the years—well, they have said a couple of things about sometimes they don't feel adequately represented on workforce investment boards. I think we have probably made progress on that.

The main point they make is "I need this skill level" or "Five of us business leaders need this skill level coming through the pipeline, and we are not getting it." Anyone else on this issue? We can maybe just start left to right. That might be easier.

Mr. Carnevale.

Mr. CARNEVALE. I think part of what we are dealing with here is there has been a fundamental change in what is required at work. In 1969, which is the last good data we have, about almost 60 percent of people who were high school dropouts were in the middle class. That is, they were in jobs that gave them earnings in the middle five deciles in the income distribution. They weren't in the bottom three, and they weren't in the top three.

Now, almost the same number, almost 60 percent of people who are high school dropouts are in the bottom two deciles of the earnings distribution. So this has been a fight. I mean, we have all been involved in this for a long time, trying to upgrade the overall skill quality.

The other thing I would say is that we have a huge mismatch problem. Most Americans are either working in an industry or an occupation that is not growing and is unlikely to grow very much and where wages are not growing. Where the jobs and the wages are growing, we are under producing talent, both through the education system and in workplace systems.

Senator CASEY. In your testimony, actually, the first line of your testimony, you describe the mismatch as between job growth and skill.

Mr. CARNEVALE. Yes, it is pretty striking. This recession, the last three recessions have accelerated this change. It is a new phenomenon in American economics, and that is that things change more in recessions now than they do when the economy grows robustly. Recessions kill off high school and dropout jobs very rapidly and institutions that house them.

Senator CASEY. Mr. Carbone.

Mr. CARBONE. Yes. As part of my written testimony, I included a chart that we use at The WorkPlace every day, which is education and training pays. It shows in the year 2008, the differential based upon education as to what the average weekly wage was and the corresponding unemployment rate.

That is the basis for it, there is almost never enough money to do a literacy program the way it ought to be done. Again, if a workforce investment board is able to coordinate all of the dollars and the agencies and the entities that offer some kind of literacy assistance in the community, you can make a lot better use of the money that is there in terms of the return on investment.

We actually have programs in literacy done right from the One-Stop system itself. We get resources from the adult ed departments of the communities of our region, and right there, when people are there to talk to their counselors and talk about careers, we enroll them in classes at the One-Stop.

We have extended it now because we don't have a lot of jobs to give out. Jobs are scarce so we are now doing it evenings. We are doing it weekends. We have done a lot more of putting learning into our system.

The issue of literacy that was raised is a very, very important one. If there is a reason for ensuring that you have a good infrastructure on a local level to attract funding from a whole variety of sources, I mean, we are always going to probably say that there is not enough of money in the system. I keep getting us back and bringing us back. The local system that this act does create is supposed to lead the system, and in doing so, there are other sources.

My remarks today are entitled "Beyond Formula Funding." Formula funding ought to be a leverage point to grow from there to bring other resources into your system to do things as godly as this. I mean, this is one of the most important objectives that I think workforce investment boards have, and yet it is one that stares us in the face. I don't think any of us can look at it and say that we are doing enough in this area.

The disconnect issue that you raise here, Senator, is one that I think we have heard earlier today and I think we will hear it almost everywhere that you go. If we are going to bring businesses to the table, like this gentleman on my left, again, the workforce investment board has to have the credibility to understand the data and to understand that they are busy people, make the best use of their time. Either you can be helpful or you can't, but don't ever put somebody in a position where they feel like their time is being wasted.

It brings us back to the point that as you move forward to reauthorize this act, pay attention to that local delivery point. We often defer that to the States, and I am not suggesting that we don't. Among the recommendations that I made is, be it the Department of Labor or another entity, to provide incentives for States to actually create a data-driven system to determine what is a region.

What is it? Are they comfortable political boundaries, or is it the economy and commuter patterns and a lot of other issues, common industries, things of that sort? There is a science to it.

When it is done that way, workforce boards are empowered with resources and minds and ideas to do a lot more and truly lead that system.

Senator CASEY. Mr. Stalknecht.

Mr. STALKNECHT. The responses were well stated by my colleagues. I really have nothing more to add to that.

Senator CASEY. Mr. Templin, anything?

Mr. TEMPLIN. I would like to leave you with a thought. A number of the Senators today have indicated their personal knowledge about community colleges and the wonderful jobs they do. Without pointing fingers, I would suggest that too often, in too many instances, the connection between workforce investment boards and community colleges aren't as strong as they need to be.

If we would think for a moment that, in effect, America's community colleges represent a public workforce system that isn't being leveraged to its fullest ability. We are considered under WIA as just another training provider rather than a strategic resource, an asset that the Nation has to leverage.

I would hope that as WIA reauthorization takes place that we look at the Nation's community colleges from a strategic perspective and not only create a place at the table, but expect them to perform. I am not sure that that is always the case.

I would recommend that America's community colleges represent a powerful delivery system in workforce training and development, that they have a responsibility and a place at the table as a partner, as a hub of the workforce system, not simply just another training provider.

Senator CASEY. That is great. If you could provide a specific change for the reauthorization that would incorporate that theme, we would appreciate that. That is why we have these hearings. At least that is the reason for having a hearing.

I did want to ask two or three more. I know we are a little bit over time, but I don't see anyone ready to kick us out. I wanted to ask a question that Senator Harkin raised that focuses on those with a disability in the context of the so-called One-Stop locations.

Apparently, when you talk about One-Stop places in our workforce development system, there isn't a great history on them being effective at serving individuals with disabilities, and I want to get your sense of that and why that is. If you don't agree with that, I would like to hear why.

But if we can accept that premise, why that is and how can we correct that problem in the context of a One-Stop location and an individual with a disability, why doesn't that seem to work as well as we had hoped?

Mr. TEMPLIN. Senator, if I might?

Senator CASEY. Sure.

Mr. TEMPLIN. I think too often we think of the workforce investment board in the sense that it has to be the center of everything. The One-Stop, by its nature, is supposed to bring resources together.

In fact, when you are looking at targeted populations like those with disabilities, it might make more sense to go to where the programs are that serve them. I will use as an example, as I did earlier, Goodwill International, one of the largest training providers working with the disabled.

Just as community colleges are places where lots of people come, we have learned that we have to go to where the people are. We have to deliver our systems to those places that are working well, rather than expecting them to come to us. I think that the workforce investment board as a centerpiece is a concept, but it doesn't mean that everyone has to go there for everything.

If we can develop the capability of reaching out to where the people are, where they are being successful, then it is much more likely that we will be able to serve them.

Senator CASEY. Going to them, I mean, just the question of location or access is a big part. Is that what you are saying?

Mr. TEMPLIN. The concept of a One-Stop isn't a physical location.

Senator CASEY. Mm-hmm. Right.

Mr. TEMPLIN. It is an essence of service, of integrated services that meet people where they are, in times and places that are convenient to them. Too often, we think of One-Stops as a physical location that everybody has to be at in order for anything to get done.

Senator CASEY. I was using that phrase "location." I probably shouldn't.

Mr. Carbone.

Mr. CARBONE. Yes, actually, that is what One-Stops are really put there for. I mean, they are supposed to be, under the purest form of the Workforce Investment Act, to create this umbrella entity where under one roof you would have access to a host of services, career being central, but anything that was needed to be supportive to that.

Senator CASEY. But you agree it is a problem?

Mr. CARBONE. I agree it is a problem, but I do think it can be corrected. Again, I think it has to do with the leadership of the workforce investment board, getting agencies to really collaborate.

I gave a couple of examples when I spoke earlier——

Senator CASEY. In your testimony, right.

Mr. CARBONE [continuing]. About two entities of the State of Connecticut that serve people with disabilities. Very important to us. They actually spend a day, a week at our center. Several other agencies, including the Goodwill and others, have a seat at the table at our One-Stop system.

They are brought in. They are not there 5 days a week all day, but they are brought in at particular times. The case counselors, the managers of the activities there, know exactly what everybody does, when they are going to be there, and we try to coordinate and take advantage of every program that is offered.

Senator CASEY. Do you call it case conferencing?

Mr. CARBONE. Yes, case conferencing means with the State of Connecticut, in order to give assistance to a person with disabilities, it is on a most in need kind of a basis. A discussion between the counselors from the State and the counselors at the One-Stop about what is the most in need at this moment is important. That conversation keeps the State entities tied to the One-Stop.

Both of those State entities actually spend a full day a week each at the One-Stop. So everybody knows each other. Everybody does work together. There is not conflict here. There doesn't need to be.

Now there are a host of other private not-for-profits that offer services to people with disabilities. As I stated in my testimony, we have received a number of special competitive grants to serve people with disabilities. We actually have a disability service center at our comprehensive One-Stop in Bridgeport.

Again, you need extra dollars beyond the formula dollars in order to be able to more adequately serve people with disabilities. From the One-Stop, that is exactly where it is supposed to be. Under the purest sense, people are supposed to be able to go to that one location and not just get help with career, but whatever supportive services are needed to be successful in that endeavor.

It is incumbent upon the regions to bring together that partnership. Even if they are not there in person, for the counselors to know what they can do, who does it, how it is done, and to involve our case counselors with that entity. That is exactly what the purpose of One-Stops were when the Workforce Investment Act was passed some 12 years ago.

Senator CASEY. I know we have to wrap up. Ms. Feldman, do you have a comment?

Ms. FELDMAN. Just a quick one. I also think we should recognize the disability advocates. In Pennsylvania, we have the Centers for Independent Living.

Senator CASEY. Yes.

Ms. FELDMAN. I don't think that we are really moving in the right direction by not having them at the table as part of the solution. They are on the outside looking in. I would say that there is great opportunity and potential to bring them to the table and really work together as partners as to how to address the issues.

Because they have their own workforce programs also that they initiate on their own, but if it is not part of the WIB system or the WIA system, it is not being recognized when there are some really exciting things happening. I would say that we need to focus on this from the perspective that they need to be at the table, driving this agenda.

Senator CASEY. OK. Before they kick us out of here, I better wrap up. I wanted to make a comment that may elicit written responses just in the interest of time. What I want to end with is what I might call a lightning round. Everybody has 20 seconds to make their 20-second message on what we should do, providing us the kind of guidance that we need for specific changes during reauthorization to make the act better.

I know it is hard to do it in 20 seconds, but if you can just make one quick point. Before we do that, this is something you may want to followup on in writing, or we may want to develop further at another hearing. One of the problems that we have in Washington is that we pass major pieces of legislation over time, and sometimes they are not integrated. There is not a seamless integration or a coordination or a strategic focus to major pieces of legislation.

I will give you one example that may elicit some written commentary. We are in the midst of talking about reauthorizing the Workforce Investment Act. A couple of years ago, we passed the America Competes Act, which has, as many, almost everybody in the room knows, has as its central focus, for example, the STEM disciplines—science, technology, engineering, math.

We are just beginning, through funding and the Obama administration's focus on this, beginning not just to fund it and make it a priority, but we have to think about strategically how do you make those two massive pieces of legislation work together? I am not sure that has been thought through, and if it has, it hasn't been emphasized enough. Think about that as you provide further guidance.

Let me go from right to left, Mr. Templin, for your 20-second message on what we should do on reauthorization?

Mr. TEMPLIN. Sector strategies work. Community colleges can and should be one of the hubs of any workforce system, and we need to incentivize training that moves beyond entry level and moves toward a post-secondary credential.

Senator CASEY. Thank you.

Ms. Feldman.

Ms. FELDMAN. Sector strategies work. I also believe that labor-management partnerships need to be considered as a huge resource to build capacity within the sector strategies, that we need to break down the silos between literacy and workforce development and fund literacy. We need the opportunity to build the stackable credentials connected to college credits that give credit for technical training, moving into collegiate training, and producing portable skills.

Senator CASEY. Thank you.

Mr. Stalknecht.

Mr. STALKNECHT. I would say to try to help change the messaging in this country that skilled trades offer tremendous opportunities for jobs and future growth and career paths to entrepreneurialism and business ownership. It would be about that. And yes, the cooperation with the sectors, business sectors is very, very important for the future workforce development.

Senator CASEY. Thank you.

Mr. Carbone.

Mr. CARBONE. All of these wonderful ideas and wonderful programs and certainly worthy programs will eventually make their way down to the local delivery level. Let us not ignore it. Let us provide the incentives in the act to encourage every State to make them robust, exciting, interesting, and enterprising institutions.

Senator CASEY. Thank you.

Mr. Carnevale.

Mr. CARNEVALE. I would emphasize that the real challenge here is integrating these different systems. Bob Templin represents community colleges and the post-secondary system. In a sense, it is a carrier. It is several hundred billion dollars in public money.

The workforce investment system is four. If we fund it at the level we funded it in 1979, it would be 25. It is a small institution. Essentially, what it can do that has the highest return is leverage the big institutions. If you can use the workforce investment system to get the education system, the disability apparatus, all the other big ships of the line focused on jobs, that is where my bias is, that we should use this money for building capacity, not for services directly, frankly.

Senator CASEY. Well, thank you very much.

Let me just say for the record that the record will remain open for more written commentary or both from our witnesses and from individual Senators. Unless you don't want your testimony to be part of the record, it will be made part of the record. Some were doing summaries of your statements. We want to make sure that you know that your whole statement will be in the record.

That goes for Senators as well.

Senator CASEY. Unless there is nothing further, this hearing is adjourned.

[Additional material follows.]

ADDITIONAL MATERIAL

PREPARED STATEMENT OF SENATOR DODD

Mr. Chairman, I want to thank you for holding this hearing, and for your leadership on the Workforce Investment Act reauthorization.

We all know that our unemployment rate is unacceptably high. Too many people have lost their jobs, have been unable to find work, have simply given up. These are good workers, talented and dedicated, and just as their families are suffering from the loss of the income that accompanies a good job, so too is our Nation suffering from the loss of their productivity.

In my State of Connecticut, we are seeing more clearly than ever that our economy is changing. Many of the industries that built Connecticut's prosperity during the 20th century are in decline, a fact sadly driven home with every plant that closes and every blue-collar job that is lost.

The sad but unavoidable truth is that many of those jobs aren't coming back. But that doesn't mean Connecticut's economy can't rebound. And it doesn't mean these workers can't contribute.

In fact, America needs those workers back on the job if we're to remain on top in an increasingly competitive global economy. That means we must empower our businesses—and we must empower our workforce. And there is no better way to do that than through job training.

American workers are the best in the world when equipped with the knowledge and training to take on the jobs of the 21st century.

And today, I'm proud that we're joined by a man who knows that better than anyone.

Joe Carbone is the President and CEO of The WorkPlace, Inc., a 26-year old non-profit that serves as the Workforce Investment Board in southern Connecticut.

Through its innovative use of career coaching, training, education, and counseling programs, the WorkPlace has carefully managed more than $200 million in public funds and helped tens of thousands of people in Connecticut reach for better jobs and better lives.

The success of the WorkPlace stems from its work to bring together Federal agencies, State government, and the private sector. It is that kind of cooperation and commitment that will be critical as we seek to get our economy back on track and put people back to work.

I'm proud to have Joe here today and look forward to hearing his thoughts on how we can replicate his successful model across the country.

Thank you.

PREPARED STATEMENT OF SENATOR MURRAY

Thank you Chairman Harkin and Senator Enzi for calling this very important hearing today.

Personally, I can't remember a more important time than right now for our workforce investment system.

Our worker training system is the place they can turn to help get a leg up—the place where workers can obtain new skills or increase their education levels to get and keep permanent, family-wage jobs.

And the value of our workforce system has only increased as our economy has changed.

That's because, as I have seen when traveling to many of the new high-tech manufacturing plants and growing industries in my home State—the needs of our employers have fundamentally shifted.

Today the skill sets needed by employers that are actually expanding and hiring increasingly require at least 1 year of post-secondary training or education, and a degree, certificate, or credential that has real value in the labor market.

So it's very clear today that we have an obligation as a nation to improve the systems and services these workers rely on for their continuing education and training.

We need to ensure that as demand on our workforce system rises due to this recession, we are also building our workforce system to handle the strain.

And it's abundantly clear that demand is growing. In fact, over the past 3 years the number of adults served by our workforce system has increased by 200 percent; increasing from 1.7 million in 2006 to 5.2 million in 2008.

Reauthorizing WIA is only the first step that is necessary to improve our Nation's workforce development system and meet this growing challenge—but it is a critical one. And it comes at a critical time.

So I'm glad that we have put together such a wide ranging panel and I really look forward to a productive discussion on how we can best strengthen our workforce system to meet the new realities our job seekers face.

PREPARED STATEMENT OF SENATOR BENNET

I would like to thank Chairman Harkin and Ranking Member Enzi for holding this hearing and their efforts to reauthorize the Workforce Investment Act. Reauthorization of WIA must be a key part of our economic recovery. Too many workers are either out of work or are underemployed. These workers need a workforce development system that is accessible and enables them to get back on their feet. Beyond these workers, though, all workers need a workforce development system that provides them the opportunity to obtain the skills for upward mobility. The economic realities of today mean that education must not stop at the school house door, but be a lifelong experience.

We will struggle to compete in the global economy if we do not update our current system to fit the needs of our economy. It is necessary that we make sure that American workers have the skills to take on jobs in emerging industries such as clean energy, health care and technology. In my State of Colorado, 49 percent of workers are middle skilled—meaning that these workers are in jobs that require more than a high school degree, but less than a 4-year degree.

Whether it is reforming the current workforce development system or finding new ways to connect workers to the skills sought by emerging sectors, there needs to be a sustained effort to train and retrain these workers. We also need to look more broadly at our education system to make sure we are connecting our youth to the skills demanded by business.

Last month, I held a "Putting Colorado to Work Jobs Forum." This Forum brought together key leaders from business, labor, the State workforce development system and academia to discuss how to grow the Colorado economy. One of our most important roundtables focused on workforce training. We had participants from across the State share best practices and offer suggestions for reaching both employed and unemployed workers in need of training. This helped provide both an urban and rural perspective of what the State and local communities are currently doing to train workers, as well as offer suggestions for how to improve workforce training.

Two key takeaways from this conversation were the need to have a workforce development system that is flexible and improve engagement with business. We need flexibility because the types of jobs being created in the State require different skills than 10 years ago. The system also needs to be flexible in terms of the types of workers being trained. There is a growing number of English language learners in our workforce. We need to be make sure we are reaching these workers and providing training responsive to their needs. We also need to have small businesses at the table collaborating on how best to train their current and future workers. Small business is the driver of our economy. Engaging small business will help drive results since business owners understand best what skills are in demand. This will also help to connect workers being trained with jobs that are available.

Our economy is changing and the skills required to compete are evolving. It is my hope that today's testimony and future conversations focused on the reauthorization of the Workforce Investment Act are centered on this. My staff has provided a list of my priorities to the committee that I hope to see included in a reauthorization. I look forward to future conversations about how we can move this legislation forward.

PREPARED STATEMENT OF SENATOR HAGAN

Thank you, Mr. Chairman, for holding this hearing, and thank you to all of the witnesses. I am thrilled to have the opportunity to be here and to talk about this critical piece of legislation.

North Carolina, like many States, is seeing some of the highest unemployment rates we've ever seen—in fact, we hit a new record high rate of 11.2 percent this past December. My No. 1 focus right now is jobs, jobs, jobs, and a critical piece of the solution is workforce training. I think my State has a few advantages—we have one of the best community college systems in the country, the businesses in our State are active players in the workforce system, and all of the stakeholders are coming together to make sure that we are doing everything we can to invigorate our economy, equip our workers with the skills they need, and make our State a great place to do business, However, we still have a long road ahead, and reauthorizing and updating the Workforce Investment Act will be an important step along that path.

I am looking forward to hearing more about how we can improve delivery of services, help dislocated and underemployed workers update their skill sets, and better streamline and integrate the various pieces of the Workforce Investment Act, from assistance for dislocated workers, to adult education workers with disabilities to youth training programs. I also look forward to supporting the great work that is already being done in my State, and providing the resources, flexibility and accountability so we can continue to attract innovative businesses and workers.

RESPONSE BY ANTHONY CARNEVALE TO QUESTIONS OF SENATOR HARKIN, SENATOR ENZI, SENATOR MURRAY, SENATOR REED, SENATOR BROWN, SENATOR HAGAN, AND SENATOR BENNET

QUESTIONS OF SENATOR HARKIN

Question 1. In your testimony you indicate that 64 percent of job openings between 2008 and 2018 will require at least some post-secondary education. What is the single most important change we can make to the act during reauthorization to ensure that our young people are prepared for these jobs?

Answer 1. WIA and post-secondary education and training programs tends to operate as if the Internet was never invented. The most important thing to do is to create internet-based information and counseling systems capability that connects job openings, job projections and career pathway to post-secondary education and training. With this information in hand we could provide useful information and counseling. The information required exists in a variety of government agencies but no one has connected the dots between the information and the people who need it. To do so will require a major culture change in the executive and legislative branches that can overcome the governmental silos.

The required information already exists, like books in the library existed prior to the age of the Internet. If you know where to go and are skilled in using the information, then you can get it, but if not you are out of luck. It is not simply a matter of connecting the dots in the information across institutional and cultural boundaries; it is also about creating a user friendly internet-based dashboard usable to individuals at home, in libraries, and a wide variety of government agencies, CBO's, private employers and education institutions that are interested in jobs and skill requirements.

Like most information and service systems connected to computer technology at your bank machine or on Internet, the core efficiency improvements comes from the interaction of the technology and the tools attached to it in combination with the participation of the consumer.

WIA is way too small and isolated to provide real counseling and other intermediary services that connects people to jobs and skill upgrading. The only real affordable alternative is to bring information and counseling services to the public online.

(1) We could provide the information and counseling necessary to help those looking for jobs to find the jobs that are open as well as target jobs that are likely to be open in the future.

Currently there are roughly 3,000,000 job openings every day in the United States both in particular industries like healthcare due to industry growth and across a much broader array of industries because of retirements and other reasons that cause people to withdraw from an occupation. The number of daily job openings will grow to 7,000,000 per day within 5 years as the recovery proceeds.

(2) An information and counseling system that helps those who have lost good jobs or cannot find one to expand their job search beyond their geographic boundaries and the personal and occupational networks available to them.

(3) An information and counseling system that helps people discern the marginal value of additional post-secondary education or training for improving their economic prospects.

(4) An information and counseling system that matches post-secondary education and training curriculums to job openings and viable career pathways. It should also make available information about public funding for their education and training.

(5) A system that ties wage data to education and training programs and also allows education and training program providers to figure out if their programs are generating earnings and employment. Real-time job openings data would also tell providers what occupations are in demand and what certificates, industry certifications and degrees are requested by job advertisements.

We do not have this information and counseling system at present. The information is, for the most part, available but has never been integrated or assembled in easily accessible online formats.

• States and One-Stops do have job openings data as submitted by employers but their job openings information is generally incomplete and varies in quality and accessibility. More complete data on job openings is available. Federal regulations give employers an EEO and a Federal contracting check-off if they submit full openings data to Job Central in Indianapolis, IN. Many but not most States "scrape" job openings from online Web sites. No States have tied this job openings data to post-secondary education and training curriculums using student transcripts or other curriculum data sources.

• Since the 1930's, every State has wage records data but very few (e.g. Florida, Washington State) have tied wage records to post-secondary certificates and degrees.

More than 60 million people have applied for UI during this recession and only a small portion have ever spoken with a real person. We cannot afford traditional counseling as it exists, and particularly personal counseling that offers the kind of state-of-the-art information I am describing here. Person-to-person counseling, whether face-to-face or over the Internet on Skype, is labor intensive. We already face a huge counseling deficit in our K–12 system, and jobs and skill development counseling, for all practical purposes, is non-existent for adults.

The need for these information and counseling capabilities is more necessary as the pace of economic change increase and we move through the greatest restructuring of the economy and employer/employee work relationships since the shift from agriculture to industry a century ago.

Evidence of the need for these kinds of capabilities is already evident in the rapid development of private sector capabilities in response to the increasing churn in the job market. But these service capabilities are still relatively primitive in the public domain. The private economy has already been investing in these capabilities for some time. The fee-based employment services industry including employment placement agencies, temporary help services, and professional employer organizations is already a $208 billion industry and is projected to grow by another $90 billion over the next decade as demand for temporary help grows at every skill level.

There are a variety of online job boards like Monster, CareerBuilder, etc. However, these only include a small share of job openings and do not come with any tools to match individual skills and experience to jobs, to match available education and training to jobs or to provide information on earnings, occupational skills, skill assessments or projections. Nor do the business models in these private job boards allow for development of these tools or access to them for people who cannot afford to pay.

Question 2. Iowa has lost more than 60,000 jobs in the last 2 years—mostly in the manufacturing sector. Many of the new job opportunities require workers to upgrade and advance their education and employment skills. How can the reauthorization of the Workforce Investment Act be used to encourage and support individuals seeking to obtain and advance in 21st century careers?

Answer 2. Iowa, like many States, suffers from a decline in the manufacturing and natural resource industries. But it is important to note that there will continue to be job openings in both of these industries. In the next decade there will be job openings for manufacturing and natural resource workers due to the retirement and advanced age of current workers. With the exception of coal, which will grow, all openings in these industries will come from retirement.

Ultimately, the number of jobs in manufacturing and natural resources will decline. Along with construction and finance, manufacturing jobs have taken the hardest hits in the recession and will come back strong. In the first years of the recovery job growth in manufacturing, like other hard hit industries, will appear promising. To some extent, though, the recovery in these industries is a false dawn. With the exception of finance, these industries will continue to decline in employment and certainly as a share of overall employment due to productivity growth within the industries themselves.

True job growth in the next decade will come in high skill services industries with relatively high post-secondary education requirements. Post-Secondary education will lead growth in both industries and occupations between 2008 and 2018.

• With the exception of Leisure and Hospitality Services, the fastest growing industries have the highest concentrations of post-secondary education demand. At least 75 percent of employees in five of the six fastest growing industries require post-secondary education or training.[1] These five industries include 40 percent of all employment in 2018.

• With the exception of Healthcare Support Occupations, the fastest growing occupational groups also have the highest concentrations of post-secondary education demand. Roughly 90 percent of the jobs in four of the five fastest growing occupations require post-secondary education.[2]

As a result of these shifts, by the end of the recession, we will need more post-secondary education and training for adults whose jobs in these industries have been lost, adults who will have to change their industry, and probably their occupation. The best and cheapest way to provide this, is, as I stated in my testimony, is by sponsoring compressed and accelerated programs for certificates in high-demand occupations. These programs will cut more than a year from normal educational programs and grant certificates with labor-market value.

Question 3. Can you explain further how "siloing" hurts the workforce investment system's ability to leverage resources and strengthen supports for job seekers and employers. How do you propose we break down these silos through reauthorization? How can One-Stops more effectively serve the increasing numbers of individuals seeking education and employment services and supports? What strategies have successful One-Stops employed to meet increased needs?

Answer 3. Because of its market flexibility the American economy has always created and destroyed jobs faster than any other. This flexibility is clearly an enormous part of our international competitive advantage and needs to be preserved. The job churning that comes with that flexibility has been accelerating since the eighties because of the fundamental structural changes that come with the shift from a manufacturing economy to a post-industrial services economy. The basic mechanism at work is advancing computer technology, which automates repetitive tasks and increases the value of non repetitive functions in all jobs. Jobs with high levels of non-repetitive tasks are growing and jobs dominated by repetitive tasks are declining. The value-added from non-repetitive jobs like design, management, finance, marketing, professional and business services is growing.

The iPod is an example of a product where less than 5 percent of the cost and value comes from manufacturing and the rest of the value and cost comes from service occupations.

Non-repetitive tasks create two kinds of jobs: low-wage service jobs like fast food servers and waiters and high-wage service jobs like designers and brain surgeons. Similarly, non-repetitive tasks create demand for high-level and low-level general skills. Brain surgeons and food servers at fast food outlets both perform non-repetitive tasks. So the two kinds of jobs that survive computer automation and "off-shoring" are low-wage/low-skill jobs that require high school or less and high wage high skill jobs that require varying degrees of post-secondary education or training.

As a result education has become employment policy. Our problem is that the alignment between our post-secondary education institutions and our labor markets is very weak. Our institutional silos and our politics make it very hard to align education policy, most importantly post-secondary education policy, with employment.

Prior to the information and Internet revolution we might have tried to force this alignment by eliminating the Department of Labor and the Department of Education and combining them into a Department of Human Resources. This was a hot proposal in the early seventies originating with the Nixon administration and supported by many members of the Senate who wanted a stronger focus on human resources, including my old boss Ed Muskie. But this is a bad idea for many reasons as well as a political stomach ache.

---

[1] The six fastest growing clusters and their post-secondary concentrations include: Healthcare Services (75 percent), Private Educational Services (86 percent), Professional and Business Services, Leisure and Hospitality (46 percent), Financial Services (82 percent) and Information Services (92 percent).

[2] The six fastest growing occupation clusters and their post-secondary concentrations include: Healthcare Support (53 percent), Healthcare Professional and Technical Occupations (93 percent), Education (93 percent), STEM (90 percent) and Community Services and the Arts (89 percent).

In modern times we can better align our post-secondary education and training system with labor markets by using information and outcome standards rather than governmental reorganization. It is this kind of information system I have discussed above and referred to in my testimony.

We do not want the education system enslaved to the economy. Education has more missions than making good workers for the economy; those other missions need to be preserved and supported. At the same time, however, in the knowledge economy, education is the only institution we have for preparing people for middle class jobs. Furthermore, people with no access to middle class jobs, especially those who become unemployed or chronically underemployed, find it very difficult to be good citizens, good parents, or good neighbors. Consequently, if educators don't empower people as workers they undermine their mission to empower their student as autonomous individuals, citizens and full members of the community.

It is increasingly obvious that we cannot afford a universal post-secondary education and training system at the current costs of our post-secondary system. We need to build education programs that move working students and adults into good jobs as efficiently as possible. This is why I recommend:

• Structured "learn and earn" programs like apprenticeship, structured work experience, as well as paid internships and paid work study programs for students;
• Credentialed learning that leads to both employability and further learning;
• Compressed and accelerated occupational training programs that provide credit for prior learning (CPL), integrate basic skills preparation with fast and intensive occupational training, leading to post-secondary certificates with clearly demonstrated labor-market value;
• Modular programs that allow for exit and re-entry and create transparent pathways among certificates, industry based certifications, and degrees;
• The development of blended forms of instruction that mix online, work-based and classroom learning;
• Job and skill counseling for unemployed and underemployed experienced workers and working students tied to state-of-the-art information on earnings trajectories and career pathways;
• The provision of family support including child care;
• Accountability systems for maximizing the labor-market value of post-secondary education and training programs by tying post-secondary transcript data with employer wage records data currently housed in the U.S. Employment Services; and
• Alignment between statewide, regional and nationwide online job boards (Job Exchanges) tied to (Learning Exchanges) that match job openings and career pathways to available courses offered by post-secondary institutions as well as online courseware.

In addition to these program interventions for adults and post-secondary students who are working, there is also a need to revive Career and Technical Education programs at the high school level as alternative pathways to post-secondary education and training or to industry-based certificates and certifications that make students employable after high school.

Question 4. In your testimony, you said that recessions "kill-off" low-skill jobs, changing the labor market more than in times of economic growth. Going forward, what will the current recession mean for youth, and especially youth with disabilities, who have traditionally relied on low-skill jobs? How can the act be improved to better support this population?

Answer 4. One of the ironies in the current American labor market is that more advantaged a youth is, the more likely he or she will be able to find work in part because they live in the communities where the retail jobs are concentrated. The labor market for disadvantaged youth and youth with disabilities has been in decline for decades. In order to give them access to work experience and career ladders we need to do so with highly targeted and structured programs that would provide subsidies and "learn and earn" curriculums leading to stable employment.

In general, however, youth, including disabled youth face a labor market where success will depend on their ability to stay in school through high school and to get at least some post-secondary education. All youth programs need to be guided by that developmental imperative.

In the current recession with so many college graduates out of work, young people, and many adults, understandably believe that post-secondary education is no longer a ticket to the middle class. They couldn't be more wrong.

Adults need to help young people to understand that increasingly post-secondary education and training has become the threshold requirement for middle class jobs. And the future promises more of the same.

- Our projections show that in 2018 there will be 162 million jobs. One-hundred one million of those jobs, representing 64 percent of all jobs will require post-secondary education including:
    - 16 million jobs for people with graduate degrees;
    - 37 million jobs for people with BA degrees;
    - 20 million jobs for people with AA's;
    - 28 million jobs for people with some college but no degree;
    - 13 million jobs for people with post-secondary certificates;
    - 44 million jobs for High School Graduates; and
    - 16 million jobs for high school dropouts.

Our projections forecast that between 2008 and 2018, the economy will create 47 million job openings: job vacancies, 14 million new jobs, and 33 million job openings to replace retiring baby boomers and others who leave occupations permanently. Job openings that require at least some post-secondary education or training will make up 64 percent of all job openings and will include the majority of long-term career jobs. We project a cumulative increase of:

- 5 million more job openings for people with Master's Degrees or better;
- 11 million more job openings for people with Bachelor's Degrees;
- 14 million job openings for people with some college or AA's;
- 15 million job openings for people with post-secondary Certificates[3];
- 17 million jobs for people with high school or less.[4]

Question 5. How can technology improve the workforce system? Have you seen any promising examples of technology helping the system reach new populations?

Answer 5. In current dollars the workforce system was funded at about $25 billion in 1979 and is currently funded at less than $4.0 billion. If anything, the need for workforce information and counseling has grown as the funding has declined. The only way to make the workforce system effective at matching people to jobs and the skill they need to get those jobs is through information technology. Technology allows a different service delivery model. It reduces the labor intensity of providing services and empowers the client to customize the service to themselves. Technology reduces the need to provide services and enables people to serve themselves. It is the only way workforce services can be scaled up dramatically, given current and emerging funding constraints.

Promising examples of public systems that approach state-of-the-art are the use of advanced job boards in New Jersey and New York, and there are also many others.

We desperately need public investment in the development of internet-based public information and counseling systems that connect job openings to careers and training opportunities. Developing an effective system on the national level would be a remarkably low-cost venture, costing no more than $15 million to build basic capabilities that could be used by State and local governments, post-secondary education and training institutions, community-based organizations, the military, and assistance programs for individuals with disabilities.

QUESTIONS OF SENATOR ENZI

Question 1. Many of today's workers are working in jobs that did not exist 5 years ago. How can the education and workforce development system prepare workers to be successful and advance in jobs that haven't yet been created?

Answer 1. Current capacity to project and predict job growth and skills requirements goes far beyond current government practices or their use in or One-Stops or educational institutions. The primary reason we do a poor job of connecting skill

---

[3] There is undoubtedly double counting of certificates because many certificate holders are also reported as having "some college but no degree."

[4] Job openings that require only high school or less tend to be over-counted because many of them are in low-wage service occupations and industries with large shares of part-time jobs or jobs with very high turnover. Low-wage service jobs account for about 20 percent of the jobs but only 14 percent of the hours worked in the economy. Many workers in these jobs are just passing through low-wage/low-skill jobs as part of a natural career progression. Jobs that require post-secondary education or training are more likely to be career jobs. There are many more brain surgeons who used to be cashiers than there are cashiers who used to be brain surgeons, but the statistics tend to treat the two jobs equally. For example, for every new job for cashiers that will open up between 2008 and 2018, there will be another 13 job openings to replace people who leave the cashier occupation. By way of contrast, for every new job for physicians there will only be 0.8 job openings to fill the jobs of physicians who leave the occupation. Roughly half the workers in low-skill/low-wage occupations move into higher wage categories within 5 years. Ultimately about 11 percent of Americans are stuck in low-wage/low-skill jobs.

training to jobs is that training resides in education agencies and labor-market services resides in the DOL. As a result, for example, neither the DOE nor the BLS projects the relationship between emerging jobs and skill requirements. The BLS, for example holds education and training constant in its employment projections. This makes them consistently low in measuring education and skill demand. Their 2008 data for example understates post-secondary demand by almost 13 million jobs, compared with the actual number as measured by the Census Bureau.

We know quite a bit about where jobs will and will not be. Because of advances in computer technology that allow us to scrape job advertisements and employer Web sites across the economy we can read and aggregate job openings and qualifications requested across the economy on a daily basis for well over 80 percent of all job openings. This information is being used in the private sector for a variety of purposes, but public agencies show little interest in developing it as a basic foundation for a modern Labor Exchange or to guide training.

We also know more about jobs that will be available in the near future because of data improvements. We know, for example, that jobs will decline in manufacturing and natural resources. We know in some detail about the coming job growth in health care as well as professional and business services. Our failure has been our inattention to building information systems that tie training to the employer wage records that have been in existence since the 1930s. One approach is connecting wage records to transcripts in order to connect education to jobs that exist and those who pay. And the second is to do a lot more serious work connecting job openings to the labor market and to job seekers through information systems.

Question 2. Given the economic downturn and high unemployment rates, many more individuals are seeking services offered through One-Stops. How can One-Stops more efficiently serve the growing numbers of people who need education and job training in order to be prepared for the jobs that will be available when the economy returns? What strategies have successful One-Stops used to make sure the demand from both workers and employers is met?

Answer 2. The great deficit in the American workforce development system is two-fold. The first is information, and the second is counseling. Given the size of the WIA system, it is simply not possible to provide all the counseling required by unemployed and underemployed workers or to fulfill the needs of employers. We will never have enough money to provide sufficient counseling. The way forward is using technology, not face-to-face advising, and to use technology to triage populations and reserve the advising for those most in need, and those unable to find employment through the use of information alone.

Systems that have relied on more labor-intensive counseling strategies have collapsed under the weight of this recession. Therefore, emerging best practices all begin with a core investment in internet-based information and technology.

Question 3. The labor market is demanding increased academic and technical skills. Employers are looking for formal recognized academic and technical credentials such as a high school diploma, an Associate's degree, and industry-recognized certifications. With this in mind: Is there need to change the outcome measures for WIA? Should there be more weight on completion and credentials and less on placement and wages? Is the system capable of delivering these outcomes?

Answer 3. Currently the WIA system is based on placement outcomes. Measures of outcome should be value-added measures, meaning that all measures of success should focus on employment and earnings. In general, however, the message in the growing importance of post-secondary education and training as the arbiter of opportunity is that we need to integrate labor market and post-secondary education services.

It would be a mistake to develop a system based on certificates for certificates' sake. Certificates have no value unless they result in increased employability. The best composite measure of success will measure improvement in person's prospects relative to their initial circumstances. This approach would discourage counselors from practicing "cream-skimming" by which they take the most employable and find them placements, and instead encourage them to help those who need the most help and can benefit the most from that additional attention.

QUESTIONS OF SENATOR MURRAY

Question 1. As you discuss in your testimony, if current trends in education and workforce development continue, even with robust job growth over the coming years, we will fall short of meeting the demand by at least 3 million college-educated Americans, and a growing share of Americans will be left behind with no access to the middle class.

What, in your opinion, is the single most important step we can take at the Federal level to change these trends and make sure we have the skilled workforce necessary to meet emerging needs?

Answer 1. In simplest terms, the most effective strategy is to align post-secondary education and training with employment services and labor markets. Presently there is no accountability system tying curriculums to wage records and other measures of employability. As a result, curriculums are not built on a view towards matching curriculums with job openings in occupations and occupation clusters.

Question 2. As Congress considers reauthorization of the Workforce Investment Act and other education, training, and employment policies, what are your recommendations for common accountability elements that demonstrate the labor-market value of post-secondary education and training programs?

Answer 2. The simplest and most immediately available way is to connect post-secondary education and training with post-secondary transcripts and wage records available on a quarterly basis both nationally and from every labor market in the country.

QUESTIONS OF SENATOR REED

Question 1. There are more than 16,000 public libraries in the United States, most of which provide job/career information and resources, such as access to computers so that patrons can search for jobs and file for government services such as unemployment benefits; take classes on resume writing; and access business databases. In the economic downturn, libraries are a community resource increasingly in demand, especially by those who are unemployed.

How can we better integrate libraries into our workforce system so that they receive the support they need to continue providing these services to the public?

Answer 1. All libraries, along with public and private institutions and even private homes should share in the common internet-based information systems discussed in my initial response above.

The FCC Broadband initiative is one advance that could help break down program silos, increasing points of contact so that every American can access the tools they need to connect to the job market. However, this program can only be as effective at promoting employment as the jobs-focused information sources we develop.

Question 2. There is evidence that the unemployed are opting to use their local library for services that the One-Stops are designed to provide due to location or other reasons. One-Stops are also referring users to libraries for job assistance or collaborating with libraries to provide help to job seekers, such as in North Carolina.

How can we support and expand these collaborations? Would co-locating One-Stops within libraries better serve job seekers?

Answer 2. The institutions should not be moved. The information and the counseling should be available to the people who need it, wherever they are. The information, the exchanges and the overall information systems discussed above should be developed and should be made publicly available through the Internet, to private homes, post-secondary institutions and libraries alike.

QUESTION OF SENATOR BROWN

Question. In your testimony, you state that 64 percent of job openings between 2008 and 2018 will require at least some post-secondary education. However, the National Commission on Adult Literacy has reported that 80–90 million adults do not have the basic education and communication skills required for post-secondary education or family sustaining jobs. Our adult education programs funded through WIA reach only 3 million adults annually? How do we close that enormous gap?

Answer. Given the limits on public resources, the best use of adult education funding is a part of occupationally based training programs. Too often, basic skills and adult education programs focus on academic curriculums in reading and math that can discourage potential participants. The state-of-the-art in this arena is in integrating basic skills preparation with occupational training or upgrading. Given existing resources, this should be the priority.

QUESTIONS OF SENATOR HAGAN

Question 1. Research shows that every 9 seconds in America, a student becomes a dropout. That being said, I believe that as we consider President Obama's challenge for our country—to gain an additional 5 million community college degrees and certificates by 2020, it is critical to consider the role in which community colleges can play in reconnecting dropouts to the workforce. There is evidence that many GED recipients get their GED and just stop there. They do not recognize the value of or even think that they have the option of obtaining an Associates or even a 4-year degree. What are your thoughts on ways that we can support young adults who have dropped out of school to not only get a GED, but to understand how important it is to obtain a post-secondary degree?

Answer 1. The primary way to get people interested in post-secondary education and training is tying it to opportunities for better jobs. We can encourage young adults to stay in the education system by tying job openings and career pathways in very explicit ways to compressed post-secondary curriculums that will move people toward certificates and degrees with a clear, measurable labor-market value as quickly as possible.

Question 2. North Carolina needs and wants to expand its training abilities for jobs that require a working knowledge of modern machines and programs, such as health care and advanced manufacturing. Unfortunately, it's also much more expensive to equip a facility to train those workers versus workers who do not need to be familiar with such expensive equipment—for example, it can be up to 50 percent more expensive to train someone in the field of health care. Can you share any thoughts about how we can help States pay for this kind of equipment and facilities when necessary to train workers to meet the needs of local businesses? Have other States confronted this issue, and if so, what are the lessons we've learned?

Answer 2. For the most part, post-secondary institutions are funded on the basis of their full-time equivalent (FTE) students, and most programs and the students who participate in them are treated as though they were the same. As a result, post-secondary institutions are encouraged to move students through the lowest-cost and most traditional programs. In general this encourages academic AA degrees with less labor-market value rather than occupational AA's or Certificates in high-demand fields. Those programs do not match with employment opportunities. We need funding systems that move beyond the FTE-centric one that weigh student loads against the costs of different programs, and as needed, provide additional funding to those that require more expensive labs, personnel, etc. Some States do weight programs differently, but it is a relatively small number, and this practice is going out of vogue due to the recession and funding cuts.

Question 3. While the One-Stop system appears to have the very best intentions, my State has found it difficult to offer services in all rural locations at all times. Some of the entities that are located at a One-Stop center might only be available certain hours of the day or certain days of the week. Some people in our State have started to offer virtual services to increase the availability in rural areas, and the option has been met with positive feedback thus far. Have virtual One-Stops been attempted elsewhere in the country? If so, have they been successful? What are the lessons or guidance for Congress so we can encourage more innovation like this, either virtual programs or otherwise, with the goal of increasing availability to job seekers, particularly in rural areas?

Answer 3. The use of information technology, satellite systems and distance learning programs are growing very rapidly in rural areas, particularly where in-person job and educational counseling systems are relatively rare. The great leap forward will be providing these services on the Internet, so that individuals will not have to travel long distances to counseling centers or locations with satellite hookups.

QUESTIONS OF SENATOR BENNET

Question 1. What role can business play in furthering workforce development? Are there on the ground examples of private sector initiatives that have helped to close skill gaps in our economy? Where do you think the law can be improved to foster more partnerships between business and workforce development providers? What are some ways that the private sector, government, non-profits and labor can partner in the development of our workforce?

Answer 1. The most effective training programs are those that combine learning in classrooms with learning on the job. There are ways to promote these. Apprenticeship programs are the most intensive models of this kind. One way to promote these kinds of partnerships is by encouraging apprenticeship programs to use community colleges in order to get certification for skills learned at the workplace. Another alternative is to use work study money to pay for "learn-and-earn" programs, including internships in the private sectors.

Given the coming retirement boom among the baby boomer generation, over the next decade employers will have to hire 33 million more workers. As retirements mount, this should create an opportunity to fill skill shortages. There is a clear need to align post-secondary curriculums with present and future workforce needs. Employers should play a clear goal in providing labor-market information to help form education and training policy and shape curriculums.

Question 2. Do you find the current workforce development system to be responsive to emerging industries and employment opportunities in energy and health care? Do you find the training in these fields and resources required for such training to be different? Are there training models on the State level that we should replicate nationally?

Answer 2. Job openings in energy and green jobs, including public utilities will be largely growth from the retirement of existing workers. So-called "green jobs" will total around 2.5 million new jobs by 2018, compared to 4.1 million new jobs and 3.3 replacement jobs in healthcare. Due to the rapidity of retirement, there are likely to be some shortages. The ability of the One-Stops to serve energy, health care and other industries depends almost entirely on the sophistication of their job openings data, and that quality currently varies significantly.

In general it is useful to follow industry growth but people work in occupations and skills are tied to occupations. Industries include many occupations with very different skill levels and pay levels. Hence any strategy that focuses on industry needs to simultaneously focus on occupations. Many industries that will grow will not produce many jobs. This is true both for old line industries like manufacturing, natural resources, and utilities, and for many of the fastest growing industries.

Because of its extraordinary productivity, Information Services is distinguished by its output growth and the intensity of its demand for post-secondary education more than for its employment share. Information Services produced $769 billion in output in 1998, grew to $1.1 trillion in 2008, and is projected to grow to $1.9 trillion in 2018. Information Services moved from our ninth largest industry in overall output in 1989, to seventh in 2008, and is projected to move into sixth by 2018. Information Services employs only about 2 percent of the workforce, which ranked it among the three smallest industry employers in 2008 and it will not grow substantially between now and 2018.

RESPONSE BY JOSEPH M. CARBONE TO QUESTIONS OF SENATOR HARKIN, SENATOR ENZI, SENATOR MURRAY, SENATOR REED, SENATOR HAGAN, AND SENATOR BENNET

QUESTIONS OF SENATOR HARKIN

Question 1a. You've achieved great success working to ensure the One-Stop Centers you operate are fully accessible. What types of incentives can the Federal Government provide workforce investment boards and One-Stops to ensure that the system is physically and virtually accessible to individuals with disabilities?

Answer 1a. Require accessibility; WIBs and One-Stops should be in compliance with ADAA for all public spaces.

For virtual access, provide incentives for WIB's to develop a virtual system.

Question 1b. How can we better use the workforce system to address the educational and employment needs of individuals with disabilities through reauthorization?

Answer 1b. Provide dedicated funding streams/incentives for serving people with disabilities.

• Create specific funding streams for Adults with Disabilities (AD) Youth with Disabilities (YD)
• Establish performance metrics that address the needs of special populations

Leverage Federal Voc Rehab funding to support.

• Hard cash contribution to One-Stop Service or;
• Reinforce Voc Rehab staff as a mandated partner in the system.

Provide incentives to WIB's that find creative ways of connecting the partner base.

• Solidify the system, using WIB's role as convener/planner/voice.

Question 2. How can we hold the WIBs accountable for ensuring that plans, policies and practices reflect the needs of all populations, not just those that are more easily served or are closer to achieving performance outcomes?

Answer 2. Do it! Write it into the act. Require WIBs to submit a plan and actual performance re: services to People with Disabilities. Provide bonus for good performance, and threaten sanctions if poor performance.

Question 3. It's important to me that individuals with disabilities are able to access resources and support, no matter which door they enter. How can the workforce investment system be improved to better align and coordinate services provided through the Vocational Rehabilitation system and the One-Stop system?

Answer 3. One-Stops should be required to work out specific times of the week where Voc-Rehab staff are at the One-Stops.

Use Case Conferencing as an effective means of integrating services.

Local WIBs could be required to submit annual reports on how they are coordinating service with Voc-Rehab.

QUESTIONS OF SENATOR ENZI

Question 1a. The One-Stop Centers that you operate are all systematically and pragmatically accessible. What specific steps did you take to make sure people with disabilities had access to the services in your One-Stops?

Answer 1a. We're located in, and specifically chose, a building that meets the requirements of accessibility.

Question 1b. As a followup to my first question, what advice would you give the committee, as we work to reauthorize WIA, to help people with disabilities access and utilize the services available at One-Stop Centers throughout the country?

Answer 1b. It takes a local commitment, but it ought to be specified in the act that failure to comply with ADAA could lead to sanctions. For those not in compliance, work out a timetable.

Question 2. It is my belief that the Workforce Investment Act is a piece of legislation that brings together multiple skill development and training providers in one place in order to provide such services to job seekers, help create a more advanced workforce, and help employers find employees—qualified, well-trained employees. This philosophy includes people with disabilities. What is the ideal relationship between the One-Stop Center and the Vocational Rehabilitation program when attempting to achieve these goals?

Answer 2. Some degree of co-location; Commitment to Case Conferencing; and Training of One-Stop Case Managers (and other staff) on working with People with Disabilities, and knowledge of entities in community which can be assistive.

Question 3. Certain people believe that the One-Stop Centers should be able to offer services to anyone who comes through the door and referrals to the Vocational Rehabilitation program should take place only for people with the most significant disabilities, yet the overall One-Stop system cannot obviate responsibility and must continue to work with the Vocational Rehabilitation program to assure that the individual receives the training and support they need. Would you agree with that statement? Do you have anything to add? Finally, how do we get to that point?

Answer 3. With Case Conferencing, two staff people who are expert in their respective fields reach agreement on *most in need* customers. A One-Stop Case Manager, a Voc-Rehab Case Manager, and often a Job Coach and others together develop plans to ensure that people with disabilities have access to WIA services.

It is important to ensure connections between the One-Stop and Voc-Rehab agencies because training and work are different. The role of WIBs is to make sure training is in an in-demand field, and to make connection to employment after training.

Question 4. Please describe how your organization, Workplace, works with employers, small, medium-sized, and large? How does the "WorkPlace" help employers understand the economic development needs of their communities?

Answer 4. The WorkPlace provides training funds to upgrade the skills of workers and to ensure that Connecticut employers are more competitive in a global economy. Beyond funding from the State of Connecticut we have aggressively pursued competitive grants from the Federal Government and private foundations. Customized training programs are designed to benefit both employees and businesses by enhancing the skills of workers, thereby increasing their productivity and the competitiveness of employers. Our objective is to enhance employees' performance in their current positions and prepare them for future advancement.

We assist employers in defining the goals and objectives they wish to achieve through selected training initiatives. At times this will necessitate the development of customized curriculum for individual business needs. If needed we help employers determine the skill gaps of their employees through assessments. Additionally we leverage our extensive network of public and private training providers to procure the best solution for employers.

The need for each of these services is dependent upon the size of the business we are assisting. Frequently small businesses do not have the internal resources to support employee development programs and will require assistance every step of the way. Large businesses typically have a handle on the development needs of employees but are not aware of local training providers. They look to the workforce board for quality training providers, partnership development and project management skills.

In addition, we conduct a "Community Audit & Needs Assessment" planning process periodically in which we both survey business needs and provide information back to employers and other stakeholders.

Question 5. As the demand for academic and technical credentials increase, there is a growing need to ensure that the delivery system is effective, efficient and user friendly. The workforce development system could be improved by using more technology. The system could benefit from being more cost effective and capable of continuous access. Is the WIA system prepared to deliver more training through recognized on-line systems? Should WIA be making use of social networking tools and communications?

Answer 5. In this area, like others (above), one way to encourage this would be to include in an annual performance evaluation of WIBs a question such as "how is your WIB taking advantage of technology?"

Not all WIBs can take full advantage of technology, including on-line training systems; if they are too small, they won't have the resources to support use of technology which is continuously changing.

The WIA system should make better use of technologies—including distance learning, Second Life, Skype, and other tools—which provide the ability to reach more individuals.

Social networking, used in a targeted and informed way, makes sense. Our system needs to reach potential customers (including businesses) where they go to get trusted information.

Question 6. There is a growing need for WIA administrators, community colleges, vocational educators, and students to have ongoing access to consumer friendly labor-market information that will clearly identify the high-wage, high-demand jobs, the credentials needed to secure those jobs, and the institutions and training programs that offer these credentials. Do the WIA program managers and the One-Stop operators have access to clear labor market information? Is the information specific and consumer friendly? What recommendations do you have for the development of more robust and consumer friendly labor-market information?

Answer 6. In general, available labor market information is excellent, and new tools are becoming available all the time.

One of the best (but little-used) tools is O*NET, which has a wealth of occupation-specific information. Consumers find this very valuable.

USDOL/ETA does a good job hosting webinars, communities of practice, and Web sites which promote the use of new and existing tools and information by workforce professionals. Some of these could be made available for use by consumers.

QUESTIONS OF SENATOR MURRAY

Question 1. You have talked about the need for the workforce development system in general, and workforce boards in particular, to be more flexible, responsive, and innovative. I know that you run a number of programs in your region that are great examples. One of those is your Mortgage Crisis Job Training Program that was designed to connect people to the workforce system to prevent foreclosure and increase their earnings potential.

Please provide some results from this program and the characteristics that boards need to demonstrate to be better able to develop and offer these kinds of responsive and innovative programs.

Mortgage Crisis: Job Training Program

Program metrics	Program to date
People Assessed for Program Eligibility	1,226
Training Scholarships Awarded	577
Provide Career Coaching [1]	971
Employment Support Services [2]	1,580
Financial Literacy	704
Credit Counseling	376

[1] Provide Career Coaching includes: Information on career pathways & required skills and Review training opportunities.

[2] Employment Support Services includes: Resume Prep; Interview Prep; Assistance With Employment Applications; and Referral to One-Stop Workshops.

Mortgage Crisis: Job Training Program—[continuing]

1. The only program of its kind in the United States. The Mortgage Crisis Job Training Programs is a unique partnership of Connecticut's workforce system and the Connecticut Housing Finance Authority.
2. Currently 993 homeowners are enrolled in the MCJTP and receiving services. Of this population 470 are unemployed.
3. Even with minimal recruitment efforts over the past 6 months, 780 homeowners are waiting to meet with a program specialist and verify their eligibility for the program.
4. Since the program's inception we have issued 577 training scholarships in topics as diverse as Health Care, Office Management, IT, Cosmetology and Financial Services. Of the 577 (380 completed, 58 did not complete, 139 training is ongoing).
5. Even with the current high unemployment rate, 78 homeowners have found new jobs and 19 others obtained a second job.
6. In partnership with CHFA, Judicial Mediators and Housing Counselors we have helped 136 homeowners avoid foreclosure. (70 Loan Modifications, 50 New Payment Plans, 7 Participants in EMAP, 9 Sale of home)

Answer 1. In order to develop and offer responsive and innovative programs such as the Mortgage Crisis Job Training Program, boards need to demonstrate characteristics which enable them to move out of their traditional areas of expertise. Innovation is found through collaboration and exploration of new partnerships which maximize competencies of other organizations. Below is a list of characteristics which we believe have led to our successful partnerships and new programs:

1. Senior managers need to seek and find the common causes. These are issues where the resources of the workforce development system can partially address problems and with strong partnerships complete solutions can be identified.

2. When building partnerships, do not assume you know all the capabilities of your potential partners. Taking the time to learn about other organizations may reveal hidden resources.

3. When soliciting the support of the business community, it is essential to use professional practices.

4. Understand what is important for each partner and what they need to get out of the program.

5. Take the time to learn about the people, processes and terminology of partners. Spend the time up front to help their key people understand your program & their role.

6. Make room for different levels of commitment.

7. Networking works.

8. Boards need to remember that workforce development is relevant to many challenges, and potential partners abound. It is important to reach out to others and let them know what you can bring to the table.

9. As part of WIA Reauthorization, USDOL should be directed to connect the American Workforce System with Regional Foreclosure Mitigation efforts.

We The Workplace will be happy to help.

Question 2. To what extent has being a non-profit, 501(c)(3) organization helped or hindered you in your work and in meeting your goals?

Answer 2. Being a non-profit 501(c)(3) has helped The WorkPlace, Inc. tremendously. It provides the flexibility to raise funds, easily subcontract with partners, and develop additional programs to meet the needs of participants.

For example, we solicit private funding for "WorkPlace Scholarships" and other programs. This has generated value-added of more than $7 million over the past 13 years, creating incremental training opportunities.

A non-profit has fewer limitations and can use Federal funds as leverage to create a larger system.

The act should provide incentives for States and regions to move the system to 501(c)(3)'s.

Question 3. As Congress considers reauthorization of the Workforce Investment Act, what specific recommendations do you have for building the system's capacity to respond to a changing economic climate?

Answer 3. This question is at the heart of the system. There needs to be a direct relationship between formula funding and the economic situation—more real-time vs. the current lag (of at least a year). Funding needs to be more closely "on-track" with conditions.

For example, current economic conditions are quite different from those considered in the act. The infusion from ARRA, when cutoff, will leave the system facing a "steep cliff."

Base line numbers could be established, then the key elements of capacity for One-Stops adjusted (with supportive funding) in response to changing conditions: Space, Staff, and Services (the "3S's"). Set benchmarks for WIBs to ensure adequate resources to meet training and job search needs.

QUESTIONS OF SENATOR REED

Question 1. There are more than 16,000 public libraries in the United States, most of which provide job/career information and resources, such as access to computers so that patrons can search for jobs and file for government services such as unemployment benefits; take classes on resume writing; and access business databases. In the economic downturn, libraries are a community resource increasingly in demand, especially by those who are unemployed.

How can we better integrate libraries into our workforce system so that they receive the support they need to continue providing these services to the public?

Answer 1. Natural integration opportunities include distance learning (e.g. One-Stop workshops shown at libraries via streaming video) and One-Stop staff located at libraries.

Question 2. There is evidence that the unemployed are opting to use their local library for services that the One-Stops are designed to provide due to location or other reasons. One-Stops are also referring users to libraries for job assistance or collaborating with libraries to provide help to job seekers, such as in North Carolina.

How can we support and expand these collaborations? Would co-locating One-Stops within libraries better serve job seekers?

Answer 2. Consider requiring (as part of WIB annual performance report) an update on the WIB's/One-Stops' interaction with/connection to libraries.

Continued partnership building is the most likely way to identify specific arrangements which could benefit each community.

QUESTIONS OF SENATOR HAGAN

Question 1. Research shows that every 9 seconds in America, a student becomes a dropout. That being said, I believe that as we consider President Obama's challenge for our country—to gain an additional 5 million community college degrees and certificates by 2020, it is critical to consider the role in which community colleges can play in reconnecting dropouts to the workforce. There is evidence that many GED recipients get their GED and just stop there. They do not recognize the value of or even think that they have the option of obtaining an Associates or even a 4-year degree. What are your thoughts on ways that we can support young adults who have dropped out of school to not only get a GED, but to understand how important it is to obtain a post-secondary degree.

Answer 1. We need to provide continued exposure to careers and earning potential (Bureau of Labor Statistics data on how "Education Pays" and insulates you from unemployment is compelling to most youth.) In addition, key elements include mentors from business, opportunities for work experience (Summer Youth programs are very important here), and project-based learning.

WIB accountability could include: "what is your WIB doing to recruit and connect these youth?" and "what is your WIB doing to keep the issue of dropouts on the agenda of your community?"

Question 2. North Carolina needs and wants to expand its training abilities for jobs that require a working knowledge of modern machines and programs, such as health care and advanced manufacturing. Unfortunately, it's also much more expensive to equip a facility to train those workers versus workers who do not need to be familiar with such expensive equipment—for example, it can be up to 50 percent more expensive to train someone in the field of health care. Can you share any thoughts about how we can help States pay for this kind of equipment and facilities when necessary to train workers to meet the needs of local businesses? Have other States confronted this issue, and if so, what are the lessons we've learned?

Answer 2. No comment.

Question 3. While the One-Stop system appears to have the very best intentions, my State has found it difficult to offer services in all rural locations at all times. Some of the entities that are located at a One-Stop Center might only be available certain hours of the day or certain days of the week. Some people in our State have started to offer virtual services to increase the availability in rural areas, and the option has been met with positive feedback thus far. Have virtual One-Stops been attempted elsewhere in the country? If so, have they been successful? What are the lessons or guidance for Congress so we can encourage more innovation like this, either virtual programs or otherwise, with the goal of increasing availability to job seekers, particularly in rural areas?

Answer 3. No comment.

QUESTIONS OF SENATOR BENNET

Question 1a. What role can business play in furthering workforce development?

Answer 1a. Businesses can participate on WIB Boards and committees. Their input is critical in developing curricula and competency models, ensuring relevance of education and training to their needs. They can participate by providing opportunities for work experience, including internships and apprenticeships. Businesses can help with early exposure to careers through School-to-Career and other programs.

Question 1b. Are there on the ground examples of private sector initiatives that have helped to close skill gaps in our economy?

Answer 1b. In Connecticut, insurance and financial service organizations made significant contributions to the development of the Insurance and Financial Services Center for Educational Excellence (IFF CEE) which was created through a high-growth grant award from the U.S. Department of Labor. Business leaders gave their time and expertise by participating on committees that created Connecticut's first 2-year associates degree in Insurance and Financial Services. Essential to this effort was the input of senior managers who saw the value of creating a pipeline where workers could enter and move up career ladders.

Question 1c. Where do you think the law can be improved to foster more partnerships between business and workforce development providers?

Answer 1c. Business partnerships as part of service delivery should be a key measure for WIB performance.

Larger, stronger WIBs with more of a regional focus are better positioned to demonstrate the value of the local delivery system to businesses and other providers.

Question 1d. What are some ways that the private sector, government, non-profits and labor can partner in the development of our workforce?

Answer 1d. Regional initiatives (like WIRED) and sector-based initiatives provide excellent reasons to partner—developing a talent pipeline and enhancing competitiveness. Major initiatives should invite all these stakeholders "into the tent" and define meaningful roles for each, in relation to the challenge/opportunity in focus. Education is another critical partner for most workforce development initiatives.

Question 2a. Do you find the current workforce development system to be responsive to emerging industries and employment opportunities in energy and health care?

Answer 2a. Yes, to the extent possible. In the health care field, a significant portion of ITA dollars are used to train individuals in entry-level health care occupations (Certified Nursing Asst.; Patient Care technician). It is difficult to move people along a career ladder to mid-level positions because of the length of programs (WIA ITA's are focused on short-term training that must result in a nationally-recognized credential) and the significant educational gap among participants. WIA funding is not conducive to remedial education courses.

In energy, there are a number of courses and certifications that are being developed as we focus more on "Green" occupations. The workforce system is definitely responding well, in large part due to the separate funding streams that have provided dedicated funding—such as, Pathways Out of Poverty (Dept of Labor); Weatherization (Dept of Energy). The system, including both private and non-profit training providers, responds to the market. It is responding to opportunities in energy and health care in a somewhat fragmented, localized way, but it is responding.

WIBs serve as regional planning entities; with relatively little money, our job is to run a system with a multitude of partners, many of which have money for specific populations and needs. Planning for emerging needs is essential to shifting supply to meet demand. The "responsiveness of the system to emerging needs" should be a key measure for WIBs, separate and beyond One-Stop performance measures.

Question 2b. Do you find the training in these fields and resources required for such training to be different?

Answer 2b. Yes, many of the energy or green jobs training program are short-term by nature and provide many options for those with barriers and/or limited education. In the healthcare arena, additional resources are necessary to bring many participants to the educational level that's necessary to move into higher levels (i.e., nursing and allied health occupations).

Question 2c. Are there training models on the State level that we should replicate nationally?

Answer 2c. USDOL is in the best position to identify best practices and create a process for replication. This is a value-added role and might be formalized as an "after-grant" activity.

In addition, intermediaries have emerged in support of "sector-based" initiatives and "regional" development initiatives. These could be encouraged, with linkage to government as appropriate. There are not particular barriers to knowledge-sharing, but it needs a point of coordination.

RESPONSE OF PAUL STALKNECHT TO QUESTIONS OF SENATOR HARKIN, SENATOR ENZI, SENATOR MURRAY, SENATOR REED, SENATOR BROWN, SENATOR HAGAN, AND SENATOR BENNET

QUESTIONS OF SENATOR HARKIN

Question 1. How can the act be changed to improve and encourage broad support and participation from the business community? What role can business play in helping workers, especially out-of-school or disadvantaged youth, develop the skills and experiences needed to gain and advance in 21st Century careers?

Answer 1. In my view, the business community wants to see an optimized workforce development system through the Workforce Investment Act. Small business owners don't always have the resources to be active participants on Workforce Investment Boards, but they can participate in other ways. For example, many small business owners in the HVACR industry employ apprentices from local apprenticeship programs and community colleges. The act could strengthen this arrangement so that more prospective HVACR technicians could find on-the-job training and a potential future employer.

Question 2. In what ways should "on-the-job" training, apprenticeships, and other supported employment opportunities be included in the reauthorization? What should we do to ensure that students are able to access the educational and career training and supports needed to be successful in the 21st century labor market?

Answer 2. Technicians in the HVACR industry need on-the-job training to compliment their classroom studies. Incentives to small businesses to provide on-the-job training as part of an apprenticeship program or an associate's degree would create more opportunities for education and career training. A common complaint from employers is that recent graduates from community colleges lack the ability to be placed in the field right away. If the Federal Government made funding or incentives available to support on-the-job training with local contractors in the trade, trainees would be able to hit the ground running.

Question 3. How would a new emphasis on on-the-job training help individuals with disabilities enter into and succeed in the workforce? Are there examples of apprenticeship programs that do a good job of integrating and supporting individuals with disabilities?

Answer 3. The general and detailed work activities required of HVACR technicians may prevent some individuals with certain disabilities from performing those tasks. I am not aware of any examples of apprenticeship programs that integrate and support individuals with disabilities.

Question 4. What changes can we make in reauthorization to address the unique needs for small and rural businesses?

Answer 4. Congress should consider assisting small businesses that develop their own in-house training programs, especially in rural areas where alternatives may not exist. Several ACCA member companies that qualify as small businesses have created their own apprenticeship programs with rigorous standards that are recognized and certified by the Department of Labor. These are especially critical in rural areas where trainees may not have access to an associate's degree. I would recommend Congress provide financial support to small business and trade association apprenticeship programs. And I would encourage an effort to streamline the approval process for certification.

QUESTIONS OF SENATOR ENZI

Question 1. In the air conditioning industry what are the common knowledge and skill gaps for those workers entering the industry for the first time? How has your industry worked with community colleges and other training providers to make sure entrants are prepared?

Answer 1. On-the-job training is crucial since a trained technician will face many different kinds of HVACR systems and problems in the field. Many contractors have found new recruits that lack on-the-job training are not ready to work on their own. The apprenticeship programs developed and managed by ACCA chapters work with local community colleges to provide slots for students to work as apprentices. On-the-job training is part of the curriculum and a requirement in order to earn a certificate.

Question 2. As a former small business owner, I believe it is critical for small businesses to attract, retain, and grow a skilled workforce. What role can business play in helping workers get the skills they need to grow and advance in the workforce?

Answer 2. Along with providing on-the-job technical training, apprenticeship with small businesses can expose trainees to the skills it takes to run a business. Too many graduates of an apprenticeship program or certificate program excel at the technical side of the HVACR business, but lack the accounting, management, and finance skills to succeed. Future programs could include programs to teach these skills.

QUESTIONS OF SENATOR MURRAY

Question 1a. I believe apprenticeships are one of the most under-utilized resources we have to prepare workers for careers with good wages, benefits and long-term prospects for stable employment.

Based on your experience, how can we improve apprenticeships?

Answer 1a. Congress can support the apprenticeships offered through specialty trade organizations like ACCA at the chapter level. One common complaint by program administrators is compliance with Federal paperwork and recordkeeping requirements for certification. Apprenticeship program administrators must jump through many bureaucratic hoops to gain approval from State and Federal agencies, including the Department of Labor and the Veterans Administration. What's needed is a change in policy to streamline the process for start up programs and those already in existence.

Question 1b. How can we use apprenticeships better in rural areas?

Answer 1b. To facilitate apprenticeships in outlying areas, the government should partner with trade associations and rural small businesses that want to provide apprenticeships and training. ACCA chapters and members have found success in attracting interested students to these apprenticeships and training programs. In many places, the number of applicants outnumbers the slots available.

Question2. Where do your members most often turn to get the training and education their employees need?

Answer 2. In the HVACR industry, contractors turn to local chapter apprenticeship programs and community colleges for training and education.

QUESTIONS OF SENATOR REED

Question 1. There are more than 16,000 public libraries in the United States, most of which provide job/career information and resources, such as access to computers so that patrons can search for jobs and file for government services such as unemployment benefits; take classes on resume writing; and access business databases. In the economic downturn, libraries are a community resource increasingly in demand, especially by those who are unemployed.

How can we better integrate libraries into our workforce system so that they receive the support they need to continue providing these services to the public?

Answer 1. The answer may be to integrate the workforce system so that more library patrons can access information online.

Question 2. There is evidence that the unemployed are opting to use their local library for services that the One-Stops are designed to provide due to location or other reasons. One-Stops are also referring users to libraries for job assistance or collaborating with libraries to provide help to job seekers, such as in North Carolina.

How can we support and expand these collaborations? Would co-locating One-Stops within libraries better serve job seekers?

Answer 2. Again, making more information available online and simplifying the information so that anyone can access it quickly and easily.

QUESTION OF SENATOR BROWN

Question. What are some ways that our Workforce Investment Act System could better meet the employment needs of small businesses?

Answer. Small businesses don't always have the resources to integrate or fully utilize the programs created under the Workforce Investment Act system. There appears to be a disconnect between the potential employers in the specialty trades and workers looking for a career. Apprenticeship and training programs that require on-the-job training with a contractor often lead to a job offer from the contractor.

QUESTIONS OF SENATOR HAGAN

Question 1. Research shows that every 9 seconds in America, a student becomes a dropout. That being said, I believe that as we consider President Obama's challenge for our country—to gain an additional 5 million community college degrees and certificates by 2020, it is critical to consider the role in which community colleges can play in reconnecting dropouts to the workforce. There is evidence that many GED recipients get their GED and just stop there. They do not recognize the value of or even think that they have the option of obtaining an Associates or even a 4-year degree. What are your thoughts on ways that we can support young adults who have dropped out of school to not only get a GED, but to understand how important it is to obtain a post-secondary degree?

Answer 1. First, Congress needs to create Federal policies that change the "culture" of job training and career counseling. The HVACR industry should be an attractive and rewarding option for those who do not seek a degree beyond secondary school. While you need certain skill levels and a base educational foundation to work in the HVACR industry, you don't need a 4-year college degree. In the last few decades, it seems our society has denigrated the skilled trades in favor of 4-year colleges. Government policy and cultural shifts have created a world where young people "look down" on the skilled trades that still offer tremendous opportunity, job security, a comfortable lifestyle, and a career path to entrepreneurialism and business ownership.

Question 2. North Carolina needs and wants to expand its training abilities for jobs that require a working knowledge of modern machines and programs, such as health care and advanced manufacturing. Unfortunately, it's also much more expensive to equip a facility to train those workers versus workers who do not need to be familiar with such expensive equipment—for example, it can be up to 50 percent more expensive to train someone in the field of health care. Can you share any thoughts about how we can help States pay for this kind of equipment and facilities when necessary to train workers to meet the needs of local businesses? Have other States confronted this issue, and if so, what are the lessons we've learned?

Answer 2. An HVACR technician needs on-the-job training in order to succeed. There are thousands of contractors across America willing to open their doors to apprentices in community colleges and other training programs. This arrangement does not require extra facilities with expensive equipment.

Question 3. While the One-Stop system appears to have the very best intentions, my State has found it difficult to offer services in all rural locations at all times. Some of the entities that are located at a One Stop Center might only be available certain hours of the day or certain days of the week. Some people in our State have started to offer virtual services to increase the availability in rural areas, and the option has been met with positive feedback thus far. Have virtual One-Stops been attempted elsewhere in the country? If so, have they been successful? What are the lessons or guidance for Congress so we can encourage more innovation like this, either virtual programs or otherwise, with the goal of increasing availability to job seekers, particularly in rural areas?

Answer 3. ACCA cannot speak to the questions of the success of the virtual One-Stop Career Centers but our experience with online webinars and other training has shown increasing acceptance in the HVACR industry.

QUESTIONS OF SENATOR BENNET

Question 1. What role can business play in furthering workforce development? Are there on the ground examples of private sector initiatives that have helped to close skill gaps in our economy? Where do you think the law can be improved to foster more partnerships between business and workforce development providers? What are some ways that the private sector, government, non-profits and labor can partner in the development of our workforce?

Answer 1. Many small businesses in the HVACR industry have created successful apprenticeship programs that are certified by the Department of Labor. The same is true for local chapters of ACCA. The curriculums require classroom and on-the-job training. In some cases, the programs work with local community colleges and participants can earn a 2-year certificate or a 4-year degree. Yet these small businesses and local organizations get little or no help from the State or Federal Governments. The Workforce Investment Act needs to encourage these programs, especially in rural areas, where there may not be alternatives.

Question 2. Do you find the current workforce development system to be responsive to emerging industries and employment opportunities in energy and health care? Do you find the training in these fields and resources required for such training to be different? Are there training models on the State level that we should replicate nationally?

Answer 2. The HVACR industry is on the forefront of the energy efficiency movement since so much residential and commercial energy consumption is used for heating, cooling, and ventilation. As new energy efficient technologies emerge, the training will have to keep up. To provide the level of energy savings promised by new HVAC equipment, the actual installation in the field must be accurately and professionally executed.

RESPONSE BY CHERYL FELDMAN TO QUESTIONS OF SENATOR HARKIN, SENATOR ENZI, SENATOR MURRAY, SENATOR REED, SENATOR BROWN, SENATOR HAGAN, AND SENATOR BENNET

QUESTIONS OF SENATOR HARKIN

Question 1. 1199C is a shining example of how resources and partners can be leveraged to provide job seekers with education and career pathways that are seamless, comprehensive, and lead to good jobs (those with family sustaining wages and opportunities for advancement). How can we support and strengthen education and career pipelines that provide opportunities for individuals, especially individuals with barriers to employment, to obtain and advance in 21st century careers?

Answer 1. A major barrier to employment is low literacy skills that prevent individuals from accessing education and training opportunities connected to career pathways. Individuals with barriers to employment often need support from adult education programs to address their literacy needs, and they need support from skills training programs to provide them with the skills needed by employers. Below I describe policies that would better align the adult education and workforce systems to provide job seekers with a more seamless experience that addresses both their literacy and job training needs. Individuals with barriers to employment also need programs that include a strong counseling component, which is usually not possible given the current funding constraints. Job seekers with challenging barriers will have much greater success if programmatic funding allows for high quality educational programming along with fiscal support for full time counselors/career coaches.

There are many things that can be done to strengthen education and career pipelines by better aligning K–12 education, adult basic education, occupational training, and higher education to allow individuals to move more easily across programs and between institutions. One immediate opportunity to address this issue is to include policies that better align title I (occupation training) and title II (adult and family literacy) in the reauthorization of the Workforce Investment Act. Such policies include:

Title I

Clarify that the focus of the program should be on the provision of high quality education, training and related services which provide individuals with the necessary skills and experience to access jobs that pay family-supporting wages and have advancement potential.

• Eliminate the "sequence of services" provisions and allow individuals to immediately access needed services;

• Establish a required percentage (consistent with current averages) of WIA formula funding that must be spent by States and localities on worker services, with an emphasis on training; and

- Clarify that WIA funds can be used in conjunction with Pell grants to ensure that low-income students receive the full support they need to succeed in training.

Increase the focus and capacity to serve individuals who have limited skills or have other barriers to economic success.

- Ensure that lower-skill individuals have a priority of service for education, training and related services; and
- Allow local areas the flexibility to provide training through Individual Training Accounts (ITAs) or contract training, as appropriate.

Revamp the current performance measurement system.

- Require use of an empirically supportable methodology to adjust performance levels based on participant characteristics and labor-market conditions;
- Review and revise current performance measures to encourage provision of services to individuals who have limited skills or have barriers to employment; and
- Develop and, over time, implement a system of shared accountability across workforce and other education and training programs.

Improve coordination between the workforce development and adult education systems and promote better integration of occupational training, basic skills, and English language services.

- Require States to set targets that steadily increase over time the percentage of participants co-enrolled in WIA titles I and II.

Title II

Set the purpose of title II to assist students to attain career and post-secondary success.

- Explicitly allow the three required local activities funded by title II—Adult education and literacy services (including workplace literacy services), Family literacy services, and English literacy services to be provided before or in combination with work or post-secondary education and training and recognize that program strategies can include, but are not limited to, approaches that integrate basic skills and post-secondary education and training content or which may dual or concurrently enroll students in basic skills and post-secondary education and training.

Mandate that a portion of federally funded title II State grants be used for seeding and scaling up approaches that integrate basic skills and post-secondary education and training or which dual or concurrently enroll students in basic skills and post-secondary education and training.

Expand work-based literacy and increase access to adult education for lower-skilled incumbent workers in other ways—for example, through flexible delivery modes, including weekend, compressed, or accelerated formats, and technology-based strategies.

Question 2. What are your recommendations for improving labor-management partnership participation in the workforce investment system?

Answer 2. Labor management partnerships are usually multi-employer industry partnerships (although they sometimes involve only one large employer) that support and provide workforce programs which simultaneously meet employer and worker needs. Like workforce intermediaries, they engage both large and small employers. These partnerships have the capacity to develop and implement large-scale workforce interventions. In general, more long-term initiatives will enable labor management partnerships to build capacity to create larger interventions with greater opportunity for sustainability. My recommendations for improving labor-management partnership participation in the workforce investment system are as follows:

(1) Create incentives for career ladder education for newly placed workers that continues post-employment by incentivizing educational providers to offer programs that meet at the times and locations that are accessible to the working adult. Workers would be able to take an entry level position while continuing to train for better paid and more skilled jobs. This approach of supporting ongoing workforce development would not only benefit job seekers but also provide opportunities to incumbent workers to move up a career ladder while creating room for new workers to begin employment. (2) Create labor management partnership demonstration projects that support capacity building in connecting the unemployed and dislocated workers to industry-based career ladder opportunities and simultaneously allow for low-wage workers to advance. (3) Create more opportunities for multi-employer, sector-based education and employment projects. (4) Create more opportunities for addressing the education and training needs of low-wage and mid-wage incumbent workers with the goal of helping them access career advancement opportunities at the same

time that employers' needs for a high-skilled workforce are addressed. (5) Create incentives for the development of new labor/management partnerships as one way of expanding industry-based training and education. (6) Support the National AFL–CIO (Working for America Institute) to provide technical assistance and other capacity building support that enables labor management partnerships to participate more fully in the workforce investment system.

Question 3. How has your partnership with the Workforce Investment Board been beneficial or meaningful? How can we improve the climate for WIB partnerships in reauthorizing the law?

Answer 3. Our partnership with the WIB has been extremely beneficial in Philadelphia. As a result of the efforts of the WIB, the RCEP, and the Youth Council, public agencies, private agencies, and businesses have aligned to create a system to address the needs of youth (Project U–Turn), of adults with literacy needs (EXCEL Philadelphia), and adults without degrees (Graduate! Philadelphia). The District 1199C Training & Upgrading Fund has actively supported and engaged with each of these initiatives. We are attempting to build seamless delivery systems in lieu of the fragmented systems that have existed for decades. Under the leadership of Mayor Nutter, we are working together as a city to bring the resources to bear that will halve our high school dropout rate and double our college graduation rate. In reauthorizing WIA, it would be beneficial for WIB's to be viewed as responsible for the workforce system rather than a single set of services, and therefore focused on building strong, supportive collaborations with partners like the District 1199C Training & Upgrading Fund to achieve strategic goals that address the workforce needs of the local community.

QUESTION OF SENATOR ENZI

Question. There are approximately 30 million Americans who have not completed high school and 58 million who have completed high school but have no post-secondary education credential. Is the WIA system capable of providing services to these 88 million people? Is the WIA system capable of providing more academic remediation, or high school degrees? Is the system prepared to focus on industry recognized certifications? If not, what are the legislative or regulatory constraints? What are the fiscal constraints?

Answer. When WIA passed in 1998, there was a promise of additional resources to support implementation. Those resources did not materialize, and in real dollars, we have seen a 47.1 percent reduction in Pennsylvania's WIA appropriation since 2002. (In non-inflation adjusted dollars, the percent reduction is 35.2 percent.) At the same time, the gap has significantly widened between where people are (in terms of literacy levels, occupational skills, and degrees) and what businesses need to compete in a global economy. These are simply realities the system faces. So in my estimation, the idea that we can achieve efficiencies sufficient to offset these losses and fundamentally expand services into new areas while maintaining all current functions may be unrealistic. Therefore, leveraging and aligning resources is our best path to building a human capital system in this country that is positioned to take on these new challenges.

Under current funding levels, of course, it is not possible for the WIA system to provide services to the 88 million adults currently in the labor force who could benefit from obtaining post-secondary education leading to an industry recognized credential, vocation certificate, or Associate's Degree. The system currently lacks the funding to purchase the education and training and supportive services such workers require, and also the capacity necessary to provide such services for so many individuals. Realistically, no system—K–12, higher education, adult basic education, or occupational training—is uniquely equipped to provide services to this population.

However, it is critical that Federal policymakers address this problem. The National Skills Coalition has documented that nearly half of all jobs in our economy now and for the foreseeable future are "middle skill" jobs requiring more than a high school diploma, but not necessarily a 4-year college degree. Another 30 percent of all jobs require a 4-year degree or beyond. This means that 8 out of 10 jobs in our economy are beyond the skills of approximately 60 percent of our current workforce. We must recognize that workforce education and training is not a "second chance" or "last chance" system for individuals who have failed in other systems, but rather is an integral part of a system by which workers in this country obtain the skills they need to enter and succeed in the labor market. Our Nation will struggle to maintain our competitive position in the global economy if we fail to address the existing skills deficit in our workforce.

The WIA system is uniquely positioned to begin to address this problem. If the WIA system were restructured, and adequately resourced, to truly serve as a "no wrong door" entry point for workers into adult basic education, occupational training, and higher education—and these systems were much better aligned to allow both integration of programs (i.e., combined occupational and literacy training, dual or concurrent enrollment, real career pathways that allow for the combination of work and learning, etc.) and seamless transitions across programs (i.e., articulation agreements, pre-apprenticeship programs, on-going supportive services, etc.)—it could function as a kind of intersection point across numerous Federal programs and funding streams and serve many, many more people.

The system is prepared to focus on industry-recognized credentials, and is already doing so in many places, including Pennsylvania. Areas that have adopted industry or sector partnership models, in particular, are very conscious of the need to ensure that workers can obtain industry recognized credentials, and work very closely with employers to develop curriculum that lead to credentials that have value to those employers. However, there is a great deal of variability across existing credentials and what has value to one employer may not have value to another. It would be important, and extremely useful, for the Federal Government to convene and advance meaningful conversations about how we determine what is a credential that has value to an employer in the labor market—and by extension, how we invest Federal training and higher education dollars. The Federal Government should not attempt to define what counts as a meaningful industry recognized credential. Just as the Federal Government does not try to define what counts as a college degree, but rather sets the broad outlines of the accreditation process, the Federal Government should strive to help set the broad outlines of the process by which employers (working with other key stakeholders such as labor management partnerships) develop industry-recognized credentials.

QUESTIONS OF SENATOR MURRAY

Question 1a. One of the most challenging aspects of our system is how best to provide education and training opportunities to incumbent workers in a way that balances the needs of employers and the workers' family obligations.

Based on your experience, how can we better provide work-based learning and on-the-job-training opportunities in our workforce development systems?

Answer 1a. Federal dollars are relatively rigid and subject to intense oversight. This can limit the willingness of local entities that are liable for these dollars to innovate. Further, much of the activity from the USDOL prior to last year was focused on finding things wrong rather than defining what works and helping others to replicate it. Clarifying congressional intent in the law would help, particularly around the technical assistance role the Federal departments can play in assisting local areas to use dollars in new and innovative ways that help people secure and maintain employment, and assist employers in increasing their productivity and growth.

An example of an innovative, extremely successful strategy used by labor management partnerships and employer-based partnerships is the use of work-based learning as part of a career advancement strategy for incumbent workers. The success of work-based learning depends on a number of factors. Most important is the need for release time or paid time for participating in an instructional program, which is often not an allowable cost within federally funded projects. Release time enables incumbent workers to participate in education and still meet their family obligations. Other important aspects of work-based learning include: preparatory, basic skills instruction along with job skills training to ensure that the worker can be successful; counseling/career coaching support to ensure that the worker is supported in the learning experience; engaging supervisors in the learning experience to ensure that the employer is engaged in the instructional design; and, connecting work-based learning to an industry-recognized credential and access to college credits. Lastly, whenever possible, it is important that successful completion of work-based learning related to skills needed on the job results in a wage increase for the worker. These work-based learning programs are often lengthy and time consuming to design and implement. Giving partnerships the flexibility to implement these types of work-based learning programs will enable workers to successfully advance in their careers and enable employers to grow their own high-skilled workforce.

Question 1b. How has your organization's partnership with your local workforce board been beneficial to meeting to your goals?

Answer 1b. Our partnership with the WIB has been extremely beneficial in Philadelphia. As a result of the efforts of the WIB, the RCEP, and the Youth Council, public agencies, private agencies, and businesses have aligned to create a system to address the needs of youth (Project U–Turn), of adults with literacy needs (EXCEL Philadelphia), and adults without degrees (Graduate! Philadelphia). The District 1199C Training & Upgrading Fund has actively supported and engaged with each of these initiatives. We are attempting to build seamless delivery systems in lieu of the fragmented systems that have existed for decades. Under the leadership of Mayor Nutter, we are working together as a city to bring the resources to bear that will halve our high school dropout rate and double our college graduation rate. We have worked with the WIB to build a workforce system rather than a single set of services, working to achieve strategic goals that address the needs of our local community.

QUESTIONS OF SENATOR REED

Question 1a. There are more than 16,000 public libraries in the United States, most of which provide job/career information and resources, such as access to computers so that patrons can search for jobs and file for government services such as unemployment benefits; take classes on resume writing; and access business databases. In the economic downturn, libraries are a community resource increasingly in demand, especially by those who are unemployed.

How can we better integrate libraries into our workforce system so that they receive the support they need to continue providing these services to the public?

Question 1b. There is evidence that the unemployed are opting to use their local library for services that the One-Stops are designed to provide due to location or other reasons. One-Stops are also referring users to libraries for job assistance or collaborating with libraries to provide help to job seekers, such as in North Carolina.

How can we support and expand these collaborations? Would co-locating One-Stops within libraries better serve job seekers'

Answers 1a and b. The greater use of libraries to deliver workforce services is a great idea, if those libraries have existing resources (e.g., are appropriately staffed and have space) and if there is a commitment at the library leadership level to these services. That is something that can only be determined locally. In addition to libraries, other excellent vehicles which can successfully deliver workforce services may include recreation centers, schools, community-based organizations, union halls, or labor management partnership learning centers. The key point is to enable decisionmaking at the local level that allows for flexibility based on local opportunities and conditions.

Our labor management partnership works closely with the library system in Philadelphia. In fact, the Philadelphia Mayor's Commission on Literacy, which is tasked with coordinating all of the city's adult education agencies, operates within the Free Library of Philadelphia. I would be happy to seek input from the Free Library of Philadelphia on your questions if you wish. Please let me know if you would like me to followup, and I would be happy to do so.

QUESTION OF SENATOR BROWN

Question. I am interested in hearing more about your experience in implementing sectors strategies. What are the key elements of effective sectors partnerships? How do existing WIA programs help or hinder the development of robust sector partnerships?

Answer. Key elements of effective sector partnerships can be expressed in two ways: those that are crucial generally and those that are crucial to the planning, design, and partnership building phase of sector partnership development.

Key Elements That Are Crucial Generally

The goal of a sector partnership is to make it possible for individuals with low incomes and/or low skills to obtain good jobs, while addressing the needs of multiple employers in an industry sector, and of job seekers and workers in that industry sector.

Sector partnerships share the following characteristics:

1. Focus intensively on an industry within a regional labor market, and multiple employers in the industry, over a sustained period of time.

2. Are led by a workforce intermediary, including labor management partnerships, with credibility in the industry.

3. Create new pathways for low-wage workers into the industry with the opportunity to access good jobs and careers.

4. Achieve systemic changes that are "win-win" for employers, workers, and the community.

In regard to systemic changes, sector partnerships focus on three areas:

- Education/training, support services, and business services (both the services themselves, and the ways they partner/coordinate);
- Industry practice; and
- Public policy.

Sector partnerships pursue three strategies:

- Increase access to good jobs;
- Improve the quality of jobs; and
- Support job creation.

Most pursue the first strategy. Increasingly, sector partnerships also pursue the second strategy. A few sector initiatives pursue the third strategy. Predictions of slow job growth over the coming decade create great concern, and sector partnerships are well-positioned to develop the capacity to support job creation.

Several success factors of sector partnerships for involving employers in an industry sector and meeting their needs include:

- Deep knowledge of industry, its culture, and employers' needs;
- Credibility with industry, or an effective strategy to gain it;
- Entrepreneurial character;
- Capacity to develop solutions for businesses and workers;
- Meaningful measures of results, and effective ways to report;
- Focus on quick response to changing industry needs;
- Commitment to long-term involvement; and
- Governance that involves business and labor leaders in key decisions.

Success factors of sector partnerships for recruiting workers and meeting their needs include:

- Deep understanding of workers' and job seekers' needs and perspectives;
- Credibility with community and labor leaders;
- Effective communication vehicles;
- Programmatic capacity to address specific needs regarding skill development and support services; and
- Influence to bring about systems changes that increase access and retention in programs and employment.

How Existing WIA Programs Help or Hinder the Development of Robust Sector Partnerships

WIA focuses resources on individuals who are unemployed. However, most low-income people are members of the "working poor." WIA should provide resources for post-employment services that make it possible for those who have low incomes and/or limited skills to advance along career paths to good jobs.

WIA limits funding for "admin" in ways that make it difficult to support intermediary services that are crucial to sector partnerships. WIA provisions supporting sector partnerships should target resources to organizations with the key characteristics and capacities of industry sector-focused workforce intermediaries.

Characteristics of a workforce intermediary include the following:

- It has an entrepreneurial culture.
- It has a results-driven focus that promotes flexibility and accountability amongst partners.
- It has the capacity to act as a project manager and to manage partnerships with multiple organizations in order to deliver services that respond to the needs of the industry and its workforce.
- It has the capacity to manage multiple sources of funding in order to meet the needs of an industry's employers and workforce.
- It has expertise and credibility with the industry sector's employers and labor, and an understanding of the sector and the needs of its employers, its workforce, and its potential workforce.
- It has or develops an awareness of best and promising practices in service delivery.
- It has or develops an understanding of systems change and a commitment to accomplishing it.
- It plays a strong role in solving the workforce needs of the industry and addressing the need for good jobs for the community and its workers.

The workforce intermediary has several specific roles in implementing the sector initiative:

• Work across jurisdictional boundaries to manage sector initiative partners' activities throughout the regional labor market within which the sector initiative operates and has impact.

• Coordinate the sector initiative's employer and/or workforce service delivery, providing a level and data-driven management capacity, information systems to coordinate the flow of services across multiple agencies to employers and individuals, and monitor outcomes for industry, workers, and job seekers.

• Improve data collection and analysis capacity, and the use of it to drive sector initiative activities.

• Anticipate challenges and technical assistance needs.

• Build the capacity of service providers to better meet the needs of employers and job-seekers.

• Bring about efforts to update understanding of employers', workers', and job seekers' needs, ensuring that service provider practices change to address these needs, and ensuring that systems change objectives do so.

• Stimulate systems change, lead efforts to identify systems change strategies and to pursue them, and monitor the sector initiative's progress.

• Bring about a structure for governance of the partnership and participate in it.

• Secure financial support, involve sector initiative partners in doing so, and manage multiple funding streams so resources can be used most flexibly to meet the needs of employers, workers, and job seekers.

• Examine possible areas for expansion of the sector initiative and its sustainability.

• Market the sector initiative; publicize progress.

Workforce Investment Boards and One-Stops may or may not be best suited to be workforce intermediaries that lead and manage sector partnerships, but the flow of WIA funding currently encourages them to play the intermediary role. Instead, WIA should incent funding of organizations that support the goal of sector partnerships identified above, and have the characteristics and capacity to be workforce intermediaries, including labor-management partnerships, community-based organizations, and others.

A large amount of WIA funding supports One-Stop Career Centers and the One-Stop infrastructure. In general, the role of the One-Stops is short-term and transactional (focused on job-matching). Sector partnerships have greater impact because they are long-term and relational, making it possible for them to meet the needs of multiple employers (improving productivity, developing the workplace as a learning environment, increasing productivity, improving job quality, and developing career paths), multiple workers (pre- and post-employment assistance, long-term skill development, advancement along career paths), and achieving systems change.

Currently WIA organizes services by groups of job seekers/workers (e.g., Adults, dislocated workers, youth). Instead, WIA should be designed to support advancement of those with low incomes and/or skills to good jobs, while reducing the division of services by category of job seekers/worker, so that programs can meet the needs of multiple categories of job seekers and workers and employers' related needs.

Currently WIA's performance measures only focus on outcomes for job seekers and workers, and their short horizons make it difficult to dedicate resources to long-term skill development for those with low incomes and/or limited skills. They also make it difficult to meet industry sector needs over the long-term, and provide post-employment services that support workers' advancement up career paths. Finally, by focusing on worker outcomes rather than addressing a broader set of issues, current performance measures only obtain programmatic information, rather than addressing systems change. Instead, performance measures should address longer timeframes, and should address the following areas: benefits to workers, benefits to employers, the quality of sector partnerships, and the impact on systems change.

Sector partnerships coordinate multiple funding sources to support their work, and States that support sector partnerships align multiple agencies strategies and resources. However, currently, WIA does little to incent coordination of other systems' strategies and resources; nor does it ease the burden sector initiatives face of coordinating multiple funding sources. WIA provisions should incent funding to align with its purpose of supporting sector partnerships that have the above-stated goal by providing for matching funds for funding from sources such as States, local governments, labor-management partnerships, and foundations.

Key Elements That Are Crucial to the Research, Design, and Partnership Building Phase

Key tasks in the research, design, and partnership building phase include:

• Convene key industry employers and unions.

• Convene key service delivery partners.
• Work with employers, unions and labor management partnerships, education and community partners to set vision/mission.
• Manage analysis of the regional labor market, including which industry sector and occupations to address, which employers to work with and how, worker needs, the union role, and capacity of potential service delivery partners.
• Work with employers, unions, and partners to design operations and systems change.
• Manage development of start-up plan and raise funding for start-up and ongoing operations.

How Existing WIA Programs Help or Hinder the Development of Robust Sector Partnerships

WIA's funding is largely tied to programmatic outcomes. As a result, research, design, and partnership building activities are crucial to meeting employer and worker needs. Additionally, sector partnerships are often under-capitalized during the start-up phase; further, funding often ends too quickly for sector partnerships to complete start-up and produce outcomes at significant scale. WIA funding should support planning grants and 2- and 3-year long operational grants. Operational grants would be contingent on achievement of key research, design, and partnership building outcomes.

QUESTIONS OF SENATOR HAGAN

Question 1. Research shows that every 9 seconds in America, a student becomes a dropout. That being said, I believe that as we consider President Obama's challenge for our country—to gain an additional 5 million community college degrees and certificates by 2020, it is critical to consider the role in which community colleges can play in reconnecting dropouts to the workforce. There is evidence that many GED recipients get their GED and just stop there. They do not recognize the value of or even think that they have the option of obtaining an Associates or even a 4-year degree. What are your thoughts on ways that we can support young adults who have dropped out of school to not only get a GED, but to understand how important it is to obtain a post-secondary degree?

Answer 1. The system has historically focused on the acquisition of the GED as a terminal credential. In order to encourage young people to go beyond the GED, the culture and mind set must be changed to embed the conversation about post-secondary credentials as an integral component and expectation of the program from the beginning. GED programs must do more than just "expose" young people to college through college tours and the like but must ensure that they are academically preparing young people to be successful in college without remediation. Furthermore, in the same way that early and middle college high school models and dual enrollment enable youth to earn college credits while in high school, we need to export these types of models to the GED system. Finally, the GED program cannot stand on its own but must include work and experiential learning opportunities as well as social supports that remove barriers and encourage persistence to and through the associates and/or baccalaureate degree.

Question 2. North Carolina needs and wants to expand its training abilities for jobs that require a working knowledge of modern machines and programs, such as health care and advanced manufacturing. Unfortunately, it's also much more expensive to equip a facility to train those workers versus workers who do not need to be familiar with such expensive equipment—for example, it can be up to 50 percent more expensive to train someone in the field of health care. Can you share any thoughts about how we can help States pay for this kind of equipment and facilities when necessary to train workers to meet the needs of local businesses? Have other States confronted this issue, and if so, what are the lessons we've learned?

Answer 2. The question here is not how you get equipment the *first* time, but how you keep it state-of-the-art, which is not a one-time investment. Would Congress create some incentives for business to donate equipment to training/education providers? What about some credit to vendors for greatly reduced purchase prices for those institutions that use the equipment solely for training? Or incentives (and waivers) to companies that allow the use of their facility for non-employee training?

Question 3. While the One-Stop system appears to have the very best intentions, my State has found it difficult to offer services in all rural locations at all times. Some of the entities that are located at a One-Stop Center might only be available certain hours of the day or certain days of the week. Some people in our State have started to offer virtual services to increase the availability in rural areas, and the option has been met with positive feedback thus far. Have virtual One-Stops been attempted elsewhere in the country? If so, have they been successful? What are the lessons or guidance for Congress so we can encourage more innovation like this, either virtual programs or otherwise, with the goal of increasing availability to job seekers, particularly in rural areas?

Answer 3. I am not familiar with virtual One-Stops. Distance learning can be used to help obtain a GED or even access skills training.

QUESTIONS OF SENATOR BENNET

Question 1. What role can business play in furthering workforce development? Are there on the ground examples of private sector initiatives that have helped to close skill gaps in our economy? Where do you think the law can be improved to foster more partnerships between business and workforce development providers? What are some ways that the private sector, government, non-profits and labor can partner in the development of our workforce?

Answer 1. Business and labor can, and in many places do, play a central role in furthering workforce development. Particularly in areas that have adopted industry or sector partnership models, business and labor are leading drivers of the workforce development system. In particular, there are numerous examples in which labor management partnerships have provided leadership in developing innovative workforce models that meet the dual needs of employers and workers/job seekers. The District 1199C Training & Upgrading Fund, for example, has served as the lead in bringing together partners in the Jobs to Careers and National Fund for Workforce Solutions initiatives. These are private sector initiatives that have leveraged private employer and foundation funding with public dollars to implement long term workforce interventions with significant impact.

Sector partnerships organize the stakeholders connected with a specific local or regional industry—multiple firms, labor management partnerships, education and training providers, and workforce and education systems to develop workforce development strategies within the industry. Successful sector partnerships leverage partner resources to address both short- and long-term human capital needs of a particular sector, including by analyzing current labor markets and identifying barriers to employment within the industry; developing cross-firm skill standards, curricula, and training programs; and developing occupational career ladders to ensure workers of all skill levels can advance within the industry.

Sector partnerships are active in nearly 40 States and the District of Columbia. While many sector partnerships are driven at the local level, some States have made sectoral initiatives a central part of their overall workforce development strategies. For example, Pennsylvania has nearly 80 partnerships serving more than 6,000 firms across the Commonwealth, and more than 70,000 workers have received training and related services as part of the program. Pennsylvania partnerships have leveraged nearly $40 million in cash and in-kind contributions from participating employers since 2005. Washington State has also adopted sector strategies at the statewide level, and has established more than 50 "industry skill panels" in 16 key industries since 2000. The National Governors Association, the Corporation for a Skilled Workforce, and the National Network of Sector Partners have partnered on a multi-year project to *accelerate State adoption of sector strategies.* The project includes a Policy Academy for States looking to create or expand sectoral models, as well as a peer-to-peer Learning Network of six States with significant sectoral experience.

Sector partnerships differ from Workforce Investment boards (WIBs) and One-Stop Career Centers in key ways. One-Stop Career Centers are designed to be universal employment and training resources, meaning that they provide services to all job seekers—and all businesses—within a local workforce area, while WIBs are intended to have broad representation from the business community. Sector partnerships, by contrast, work within a single, specific industry that has been identified as critical to local or regional economic success. As a result, sector partnerships develop a depth of understanding of a specific sector that is neither practical nor desirable for a WIB. Sector partnerships are not meant to replace WIBs—in fact, WIBs are a key partner in many successful sector partnerships—nor are they meant to offer the universal services of One-Stop Career Centers. Instead, they are designed to help a local area or region develop depth and capacity within targeted, specific industries in ways that complement broader workforce efforts.

Sector partnerships are guided by employers and often focus, at least initially, on skilling up an incumbent workforce. However, well-designed sector partnerships can also have significant positive impacts on low-income workers. According to a multi-year, random assignment impact study conducted by the public interest research group Public/Private Ventures, participants in sector-based training programs earned an average of 18.3 percent (or about $4,500) more than a control group over the 24-month period of the study. In addition, participants in sector programs were more likely to work in jobs with benefits, including health insurance and paid time off, and were more likely to find consistent work—about 1.3 additional months of employment over the 2-year period than the control group average.

A 2002 report from the Aspen Institute similarly showed improved labor market outcomes for low-income workers in seven sector programs across the country. Participants saw an average increase in hourly wages of 31 percent over the 2 years of the study period, and 39 percent of participants had been able to move out of poverty on the basis of their personal income alone.

Although Congress established a sector grant program as part of the recently re-authorized Trade Adjustment Assistance (TAA) program, this program is only available for communities impacted by foreign trade and it has not yet been funded. WIA does not explicitly support sector partnerships, meaning that there is limited Federal support for these initiatives, and coordination between sector programs and other elements of the workforce system can sometimes be limited.

Senators Brown (D–OH) and Snowe (R–ME), have introduced the "Strengthening Employment Clusters to Organize Regional Success (SECTORS) Act" (S. 777), and have advocated for its inclusion in WIA reauthorization. The SECTORS Act would amend WIA to provide designated funding and distinct performance measures for industry or sector partnerships. The bill would establish a series of 1-year planning grants and 3-year implementation grants to eligible partnerships comprised of employers, labor organizations, local WIBs, post-secondary educational institutions, State workforce agencies or other entities providing State employment services. Partnerships receiving grant funds would be responsible for meeting a range of strategic objectives, including identifying training needs of multiple businesses; helping post-secondary educational institutions and training institutions align curricula and programs to industry demands; developing and strengthening career ladders within and across companies; and improving job quality through improving wages, benefits, and working conditions.

Question 2. Do you find the current workforce development system to be responsive to emerging industries and employment opportunities in energy and health care? Do you find the training in these fields and resources required for such training to be different? Are there training models on the State level that we should replicate nationally?

Answer 2. Models for service delivery exist at the local level more often than at the State level. The challenge with emerging industries is that until you have employers and labor at the table defining their workforce needs, you cannot design tailored services (one way to do this is to engage in the retraining of incumbent workers as industries or companies morph). On the other hand, the opportunity with emerging industries is that the public workforce system is on level ground with private vendors and has an equal opportunity to develop the supply pipeline—the advantage being that populations that are the target of public investments (veterans, disconnected youth, dislocated workers, economically marginalized adults, etc.) have a good shot at filling industry's need for emerging employment opportunities.

RESPONSE BY ROBERT TEMPLIN, JR. TO QUESTIONS OF SENATOR HARKIN, SENATOR ENZI, SENATOR MIKULSKI, SENATOR MURRAY, SENATOR REED, SENATOR BROWN, SENATOR HAGAN, AND SENATOR BENNET

QUESTIONS OF SENATOR HARKIN

Question 1. What is the single most important thing that community colleges can do to help meet President Obama's goal—for the United States to again lead the world in college completion rates. And what is the single most important thing that community colleges can do to ensure a competitive workforce now and in the future?

Answer 1. The answer to both questions is the same: The single most important thing that community colleges can do to help meet President Obama's goal and ensure a competitive workforce is for them to serve as the "on ramp" for the growing number of Americans needing post-secondary education, and once enrolled, these students need to be assisted by community colleges in completing a post-secondary credential in increasing numbers. If we are to reach the President's goal, many more Americans who have traditionally been left on the periphery of higher education, must become active and successful learners in post-secondary education and they must achieve market-valued credentials. Among the target groups are recent high school graduates who would be the first in their family to go to college, high school dropouts, 17–24-year-old high school graduates who are out of school and who lack the training for a family-sustaining wage, low-income wage earners, minorities, and immigrants. Community colleges are America's best national resource for achieving the President's goal.

Question 2. How can the workforce investment system help students with disabilities transition from education or employment skill training programs into meaningful careers with opportunities for growth? What do we need to do in order to better support students who face barriers to accessing and succeeding in post-secondary education programs or employment?

Answer 2. The current workforce investment system does not provide resources to meet the needs of students with disabilities who need support and guidance to help them advance from the classroom to the workforce. Student transition from high school and community college should begin in a student's freshman year of high school with opportunities to assess interests in the context of career exploration. All students should exit high school with career and post-secondary education navigation skills that will serve them for a lifetime.

Many students with disabilities face employment barriers that make the move from education to the workforce more difficult. These students should have IEP-directed services at both the secondary school and post-secondary education levels that leverage the full array of resources from the Workforce Investment Act-funded system and community-based organizations while they are in school or attending community college.

While career navigation sets the course for these individuals, access to supports is essential to make the journey. Such individuals would benefit from the expertise of community-based organizations, such as Goodwill Industries, that have the experience and resources to help students with disabilities and disconnected youth to advance into college, the workforce, and careers. As established local stakeholders, such community-based organizations are strongly positioned to help students with employment barriers learn specialized skills required by local businesses and employers. Community-based organization's experience helping people with a range of barriers equips them to help students navigate a complex, often fragmented, maze of supports administered by numerous Federal agencies including the Departments of Labor, Education, Health and Human Services and others.

Students with disabilities and other barriers need assistance in securing supports such as:

- training,
- appropriate professional clothing,
- reliable transportation,
- tools and materials,
- assistive technology,
- childcare,
- stable housing,
- help navigating "benefit cliffs" (sudden drops in benefits like TANF, Medicaid, or SSI people experience when transitioning to work), and
- assistance in adjusting to the workplace.

It is recommended that our country establish a clear multi-system goal of career and college readiness for all students; establish a multi-systemic structure involving the Departments of Education, Labor, and other agencies as needed, that provide career guidance to youth (ages 14–24) with priority given to youth with disabilities and other youth with characteristics that put them at higher risk of becoming court-involved, homeless, or otherwise disconnected; and provide funding for this specific program.

Question 3. How can the act be reauthorized to encourage and support community college involvement with the workforce investment system?

Answer 3. The American Association of Community Colleges (AACC) has developed a comprehensive set of recommendations for WIA reauthorization. Most of these recommendations directly answer this question, and I have provided a copy of those recommendations for your reference. (Attachment A) In brief, WIA should be authorized with an eye towards cementing the community college role in planning and executing workforce development strategies at the State, regional and local levels. Customer choice, as implemented in the Individual Training Accounts, should be better balanced with other types of "cohort" approaches that prioritize the use of community colleges for training, including direct support for community college training capacity at the national level, increased use of training contracts and sector initiatives like the ones funded by the Community-Based Job Training Grants. These approaches better address the need that community colleges have to expand their training capacity. Finally, though their impact has been muted by DOL-granted waivers in many States, the subsequent eligibility requirements for training providers must be significantly altered. Regionally accredited, public institutions of higher education should be automatically eligible to participate in the workforce system.

Question 4. Iowa's community colleges are essential partners in training and upgrading the skills of job seekers and workers—for example, by providing training opportunities to soon-to-be-released inmates. How can community colleges work more efficiently with the workforce system to ensure that individuals gain access to the courses and credentials they need. How can community colleges do a better job of working with local businesses to ensure those courses lead to good jobs?

Answer 4. We must build upon and emphasize regional market approaches that answer threshold questions regarding what jobs are available now and in the future, what skills and credentials are needed for those jobs, and what skills gaps there are in the workforce. After those questions are answered, cohesive business-driven plans must be formulated and executed to address the identified employment needs. Sector-based initiatives that bring all the stakeholders together in a focused way are particularly effective structures for doing all of these things. Community colleges must endeavor to work more closely with businesses and the workforce system as they devise and refine their education and training programs, such as through the effective use business advisory boards and by having representatives on WIA boards. Perhaps most importantly, colleges must work closely with the workforce system to ensure that workers coming into the system are aware of all the tools available to them to help them access the training and credentials they need, particularly those offered by Federal and State student aid programs.

Question 5. What key challenges will community colleges face as demand for their courses continues to grow and the economy changes?

Answer 5. The overarching challenge that community colleges face is one of capacity, and many of the AACC recommendations for WIA reauthorization address the issue of how the system can better help colleges expand their training capacity in the face of growing demand. In addition, and outside the scope of the WIA bill itself, community colleges face tremendous challenges in expanding and modernizing their facilities to meet this demand. Estimates put this need at well north of $10 billion. The need is particularly acute for career and technical education programs that require specialized facilities and equipment. The American Graduation Initiative recognized this need by proposing to provide $2.5 billion in seed money for community college facilities, and there was nearly money for this purpose in the American Recovery and Reinvestment Act. Chairman Harkin has been an outstanding champion for facilities funds for community colleges, and we look forward to continue working with him to realize Federal support in this area.

One other challenge, particularly in some career and technical education programs, is the ability to hire and retain the faculty needed not only to expand, but to maintain current training capacity. There are two principal forces at work here. First, since the average community college derives approximately 60 percent of its revenues from State and local support, recent declines in this support have severely impaired the colleges' ability to maintain sufficient faculty levels. Second, in many workforce programs, the salaries offered by the industries we are training for are much larger than those that colleges are able to offer to its faculty. This problem is especially acute in the nursing and allied health fields, but it is by no means isolated to them.

Question 6. In your experience, what characterizes the most effective partnerships between community colleges and secondary schools?

Answer 6. The four critical elements characterizing effective partnerships between community colleges and secondary schools are:

• Mutual commitment of the community college and the secondary school system to students who are low-income, minority, and first generation college-going;
• Joint recognition that preparing students to be "college-ready" is a responsibility of both the secondary school system and community colleges;
• Leadership at both the superintendent of schools and the community college president levels; and
• Win-win incentives such as dual enrollment funding where both the schools and the community colleges are financially supported for their efforts.

An area where critical attention and "win-win" incentives are critically needed now is in the area of assessing and preparing high school students to be "college-ready" so they are not required to attend remedial or developmental courses at the community college following high school graduation.

Question 1. Wyoming's seven community colleges are the backbone of the education and workforce development system in my great State of Wyoming and have strong relationships with local businesses. I would like to know how the Northern Virginia Community College works with employers to make sure the community college coursework will lead to credentials and certificates that are meaningful to those industries?

Answer 1. NOVA's most powerful strategy in working with local businesses is through sector-based strategies. Currently we have three sector strategies under way: the health care system sector; the emerging energy and "green" industry sector; and the science, technology, engineering, and math-based business sector (STEM). In each of these sectors, the college president either personally leads or participates in a coalition of sector CEO's in commissioning a market demand study for jobs needed within the region. Based upon the results of that study, the coalition identifies the types of jobs where training is needed, sets targets for training and education outcomes, identifies and commits to raising the resources to meet those targets, sets the skill requirements for the projected job needs, and monitors progress in meeting those targets over time.

Question 2. In our current economic climate, the Nation's community colleges are receiving more applicants than they have available slots. What will be some of the challenges for the community college system over the next 5 years in meeting the needs of job seekers and upgrading the skills of those already in the workforce?

Answer 2. Expanding their capacity to meet growing demands is the major challenge for community colleges in the next 5 years, especially as they experience weakening State and local financial support. Many of the AACCs' recommendations for WIA reauthorization (attached) address the issue of how the system can better help colleges expand their training capacity in the face of growing demand. As Anthony Carnevale noted in his testimony before the committee, it may be a good idea to emphasize support for infrastructure more in a reauthorized WIA.

Question 3. There is increasing focus on industry-recognized certifications that are stacked (increasingly levels of technical qualifications) and that carry academic credit. This represents the growing alignment between the employer, community and the post-secondary education system. Do WIA administrators have access to information on industry-recognized certifications? Do they have access to those that are stackable and those that carry academic credit? If not, what recommendations do you have for ensuring quality data that is reliable and valid on industry-recognized certifications?

Answer 3. Many Workforce Investment Act administrators, especially leaders in their local business community and those with close partnerships with the higher education community, understand the importance of industry-recognized certifications and the alignment between the employer and the post-secondary education system. This focus on industry certifications is especially important in regions with growing occupations in industries needing workers with technical expertise, but not necessarily a 4-year college degree. But most WIA administrators are not experts in post-secondary or higher education requirements in creating those stackable credentials or the challenges in identifying and retaining students within those programs. Therefore, the need for post-secondary educational institution representation on the local or State workforce board, to continually provide that needed level of expertise and involvement, is critically important.

It is important for job seekers wishing to upgrade their skills with these increasing levels of technical qualifications, to understand how they, as a student, can work with their local community college or technical institute, to gain the certifications needed for a particular occupation. Educators must be actively engaged within the State or local workforce system to assure a broad understanding of identified credentials and the various pathways that can be followed to acquire those skills. Local WIA administrators must assure that these information sources are accessible to customers at the One-Stop Centers and that Center staff understand and can respond to questions, as needed.

Question. First, I'd like to thank Chairman Harkin for holding this hearing. Re-examining the ways in which our Federal workforce programs currently operate is vitally important, especially since State workforce systems across the country are facing acute, and in some cases, unfamiliar challenges with regard to education and training. My question is directed at Dr. Templin. You spoke briefly about how Community Colleges are viewed primarily as the "trainers" in our workforce development system, and that we on the committee should begin thinking about how community colleges could really be workforce hubs that are active partners in the workforce development system instead of just vendors. With that in mind, I realize that community colleges are facing some serious issues with regard to capacity, both organizational and physical. I know that the 16 community colleges in my home State of Maryland are receiving such a high number of applications that it threatens their ability to maintain their open-admission policies and low-cost tuitions: the very things that have made community colleges attractive for generations. We've been trying to address this issue of capacity over the past 5 years through the Community-Based Job Training Grants (CBJTG), which, as you know through experience, provides competitive grants to community colleges to train people for careers in high-growth, high-demand industries. Currently, those careers are mostly in the allied health professions, and we desperately need more nurses and technicians in our hospitals. So, if we consider how stretched and stressed community colleges are right now simply doing what they've been doing, what kinds of supports could we include in our reauthorization that would facilitate a move towards a fuller integration of community colleges in the workforce investment system?

Answer. The American Association of Community Colleges (AACC) has developed a comprehensive set of recommendations for WIA reauthorization. Most of these recommendations directly answer this question, and I have attached them for your reference. (Attachment A) In brief, WIA should be authorized with an eye towards cementing the community college role in planning and executing workforce development strategies at the State, regional and local levels. Customer choice, as implemented in the Individual Training Accounts, should be better balanced with other types of "cohort" approaches that prioritize the use of community colleges for training, including direct support for community college training capacity at the national level, increased use of training contracts and sector initiatives like the ones funded by the Community-Based Job Training Grants. These approaches better address the real need that community colleges have for the support necessary to expand their training capacity. Finally, though their impact has been muted by DOL-granted waivers in many States, the subsequent eligibility requirements for training providers must be significantly altered. Public institutions of higher education should be automatically eligible to participate in the workforce system.

QUESTIONS OF SENATOR MURRAY

Question 1. We know that increasingly people need some type of post-secondary degree, credential, or certification that has real value in the labor market to be successful in the long-term. This requires that our nearly 1,200 community colleges be responsive, flexible, and innovative. We know that you have developed such an institution in Northern Virginia.

What are some principles from NOVA's success that could be applied more broadly to other community colleges?

Answer 1. NOVA's success as an institution increasingly hinges upon its ability to partner with public school divisions, business and industry, workforce systems, and community-based non-profit organizations. The college must see its students and adult learners within the complexity of their life situations and partner with other organizations to see that wrap around support services are available. Similarly, the college must partner with regional businesses and workforce systems to create market-driven workforce training strategies that are synchronized with the business realities of the community. Appropriately executed, this partnership approach results in job training and education for family-sustaining career advancement for low-income workers and a sustainable resource of appropriately skilled workers who contribute to the economic vitality of their region and the competitiveness of the businesses that hire them.

Below are some of the principles that guide such a partnership system:

• **Targeted Audiences:** Programs target specific low-to-moderate-income adult or youth audiences that would normally be unlikely to access college on their own;

• **Market-Driven:** Occupational/Sectoral training focus driven by *local* employer needs and engagement;

• **Dual Outcomes:** The overall program is designed to track achievement of new job/career advancement outcomes, as well as college or alternative credential attainment outcomes;

• **Career Advancement Credential(s):** While learning new job skills for an immediate new career opportunity, programs build towards specified longer term college or alternative credentials for career advancement;

- **Support Services:** Partners support the delivery of non-instructional support services needed to achieve longer term life-transforming outcomes;
- **College Process Re-Engineering:** College identifies specific ways that it plans to adapt typical processes to serve the audience and program needs;
- **Academic Integrity:** Programs must meet the college's core academic standards and external regulatory requirements;
- **Integration Plans:** Programs identify specific roles for the college and partners in an integrated service delivery plan;
- **Sustainability:** Partner organizations and the community college jointly own and share the burden for resource development and/or resource-sharing plans that address long-term sustainability of the initiative; and
- **Scalability:** Partner organizations work toward the development of solutions that may be piloted in small cohorts but that can scale once the need and solution are validated.

Question 2. Your community college serves quite a large area. How do you work with the various workforce boards in northern Virginia?

Answer 2. In Virginia, former Governor Tim Kaine and the General Assembly appointed the Virginia Community College System (VCCS) as the State's Workforce Investment Act grant recipient. As such, the local workforce boards follow policy guidance from State VCCS staff along with the private sector-led Virginia Workforce Council. This type of State leadership is quite conducive to smooth working relationships between local community colleges and local workforce boards in Virginia, as policy guidance and goals are consistent and well known.

The area represented by NOVA is part of one labor market (northern Virginia) but also the Greater Washington region, which includes the District of Columbia and the State of Maryland. Workers and job seekers easily cross State boundaries in their pursuit of education, training and jobs. In northern Virginia, community college officials serve on the two (2) local Workforce Boards; one representing nearly 2 million residents and one representing roughly 300,000 residents. College representatives are actively engaged in Board policy considerations and NOVA is an Approved Training Provider in both workforce areas, in addition to the entire Commonwealth of Virginia. Because of the size and breadth of our course offerings, NOVA is usually the most active training provider in the region, receiving vouchers from Workforce Investment Act-eligible clients seeking to gain or improve job training skills. In fiscal year 2009, NOVA received over $285,000 in WIA vouchers; in fiscal year 2010, we are on track to receive $325,000.

The college also works closely with both local workforce areas on independent grant funding solicitations, either with the college as the lead applicant or as a sub-grant recipient to the local board as the grant applicant. The college has been successful in receiving Federal Labor Community Job Training Partnership grant awards and have partnered with the local Boards in program implementation. We have a close working relationship with the Boards and their respective One-Stop Center staff, which greatly expedites preparation of grant funding applications and working through any program issues.

Further, our college and the local Workforce Boards can provide complimentary outreach and services to reach job seekers. For example, the Northern Virginia Workforce Investment Board has partnered with NOVA's Woodbridge Campus to develop and provide staff for a One-Stop Center on site at the campus. This initiative has helped our college students with having career development and job search assistance on our campus and the Workforce Board has expanded its outreach and services to an important population that might not necessarily enter a One-Stop Center located elsewhere in the community.

QUESTIONS OF SENATOR REED

Question 1a. There are more than 16,000 public libraries in the United States, most of which provide job/career information and resources, such as access to computers so that patrons can search for jobs and file for government services such as unemployment benefits; take classes on resume writing; and access business databases. In the economic downturn, libraries are a community resource increasingly in demand, especially by those who are unemployed.

How can we better integrate libraries into our workforce system so that they receive the support they need to continue providing these services to the public?

Question 1b. There is evidence that the unemployed are opting to use their local library for services that the One-Stops are designed to provide due to location or other reasons. One-Stops are also referring users to libraries for job assistance or collaborating with libraries to provide help to job seekers, such as in North Carolina.

How can we support and expand these collaborations? Would co-locating One-Stops within libraries better serve job seekers?

Answers 1a and 1b. In an Associated Press news release on March 25, 2010, a study funded by the Bill and Melinda Gates Foundation for the University of Washington Information School reported that one-third of all Americans 14 years or older, approximately 77 million people, use public computers primarily at libraries to look for employment or otherwise improve their lives. The Report also noted that for families living at or below the Federal poverty guidelines ($22,000 per year for a family of four), 44 percent report using computers at public libraries. The findings from this report are important in that it shows people across all age and ethnic groups use public library computers.

In a poor economy, citizens appear to turn to their local public libraries to access information, seek assistance and look for employment. Regardless of the size of the State or local library system and its internal resources, several characteristics that are consistent across all libraries are that there are not sufficient numbers of computers or the patrons do not have enough time to fully utilize the existing computers. Library administrators also report that many patrons do not have adequate computer skills to be fully functional on the library computers, nor are sufficient library staff available to respond to customer needs. Further, many library staff are not sufficiently trained to adequately guide a job seeker using a library computer with their job search needs.

It should be noted that the Institute of Museum and Library Services has funded a grant with the State Library of North Carolina (SLNC) to initiate Project Compass, a 1-year initiative to work with State libraries in support of public libraries' efforts to meet the urgent and growing demands of communities as they struggle with the loss of jobs and the needs of the unemployed. The key goals of Project Compass include: (1) supporting State library agencies in maximizing the effectiveness of local libraries providing services and outreach to unemployed residents; (2) to foster successful, ongoing collaboration among State library agencies; (3) to promote strategic partnerships with other organizations that serve the unemployed; and (4) increase awareness of library services and demonstrate the critical role libraries serve during times of economic crisis.

Congress may wish to consider encouraging States and local library and workforce officials to align certain workforce services within a public library, possibly including designating space or computers specifically for job search and employment training purposes. In certain circumstances, workforce staff might be assigned to libraries, as affiliate workforce center sites, to meet the public where service demands are greatest.

QUESTION OF SENATOR BROWN

Question. In Ohio, our community colleges have been first responders for our communities devastated by the loss of manufacturing jobs. Colleges such as Lorain Community College and Sinclair Community College have been at the center of economic development and retooling for their regions. Ohio created the Ohio Skills Bank, which is designed to align education and job training with economic development. One of the challenges our colleges have reported is identifying the stackable certificates that employers value and reward in the workplace and that will count towards a college degree. How have you identified the credentials that are valued in the workplace?

Answer. Community colleges such as Lorain Community College and Sinclair Community College are national leaders in the community college field relating to workforce training. They would be among those institutions that understand that first and foremost, establishing market-valued post-secondary credentials must be a process driven by business, in collaboration with their education partners such as community colleges. Industry certifications are one growing trend that many community colleges infuse into their coursework, allowing workers both to obtain the knowledge and skills needed to obtain the certifications and to build up credits towards a certificate or degree. The information technology industry, for example, has been a leader in this area and has a well-developed system of industry certifications.

In other industries that are not as far along, colleges sometimes work directly with businesses to identify discrete skill sets that then might comprise modules along the way to a degree program. The institution may offer certificates to signify completion of these steps.

One other important element to this issue is the matter of what are often called, "soft skills." There are a growing number of tools to measure and recognize when a worker has acquired certain sets of soft skills. Often completion of these units will be recognized by some sort of "work readiness" certificate that signifies to employers that the student has acquired the knowledge and tools to contribute in a work environment.

Question 1. Research shows that every 9 seconds in America, a student becomes a dropout. That being said, I believe that as we consider President Obama's challenge for our country—to gain an additional 5 million community college degrees and certificates by 2020, it is critical to consider the role in which community colleges can play in reconnecting dropouts to the workforce. There is evidence that many GED recipients get their GED and just stop there. They do not recognize the value of or even think that they have the option of obtaining an Associates or even a 4-year degree. What are your thoughts on ways that we can support young adults who have dropped out of school to not only get a GED, but to understand how important it is to obtain a post-secondary degree?

Answer 1. There are two promising "best practices" that are worth highlighting in responding to your question regarding post-secondary education opportunity for GED recipients:

• **Middle College:** Middle College is a high school/GED completion program that is located on and integrated with the community college environment allows individuals without a high school degree to increase their income and employability by simultaneously pursuing a GED, community college education, and a workforce certification in a community college environment. The program offers targeted remedial courses, access to workforce readiness courses, enrollment in community college courses applicable to a degree or industry-based certificate, and comprehensive support services. Middle colleges now exist in some form in at least 20 States. In Virginia, results from our State's six middle colleges are that of those enrolled, over 70 percent of active students have received a GED; over 50 percent of GED completers are enrolled in a post-secondary education program; and nearly 60 percent of the GED completers earned a Career Readiness Certificate.

• **Year Up:** Year Up is a 1-year, intensive training program currently offered in six U.S. cities that provides urban young adults 18–24, with a unique combination of technical and professional skills, college credits (usually in cooperation with a local community college), an educational stipend and corporate internship. GED completers are eligible to participate in an information technology apprenticeship program and be paid during 1-year of learning. Success results to date include 100 percent placement of qualified students into internships, 83 percent student retention, 90 percent of interns meet internship partner expectations, and 87 percent of graduates are placed in full- or part-time positions within 4 months of graduation with $15 per hour average wage at placement.

Question 2. North Carolina needs and wants to expand its training abilities for jobs that require a working knowledge of modern machines and programs, such as health care and advanced manufacturing. Unfortunately, it's also much more expensive to equip a facility to train those workers versus workers who do not need to be familiar with such expensive equipment—for example, it can be up to 50 percent more expensive to train someone in the field of health care. Can you share any thoughts about how we can help States pay for this kind of equipment and facilities when necessary to train workers to meet the needs of local businesses? Have other States confronted this issue, and if so, what are the lessons we've learned?

Answer 2. What you have described, unfortunately, is the ongoing experience of most of America's community colleges. Federal programs from the Department of Education, National Science Foundation, and the Department of Labor's Community-Based Job Training Grants have been helpful, but woefully inadequate. In some communities, industry sector companies and organizations have teamed with local community colleges to make one-time purchases of expensive equipment and construction of facilities. In other instances, turning to the uses of technology-based simulations (expensive pieces of equipment themselves) have been options used. More typically though, most community colleges find themselves either using dated equipment and facilities or facing the reduction of programs requiring such specialized expenditures.

Question 3. While the One-Stop system appears to have the very best intentions, my State has found it difficult to offer services in all rural locations at all times. Some of the entities that are located at a One-Stop Center might only be available certain hours of the day or certain days of the week. Some people in our State have started to offer virtual services to increase the availability in rural areas, and the option has been met with positive feedback, thus far. Have virtual One-Stops been attempted elsewhere in the country? If so, have they been successful? What are the lessons or guidance for Congress so we can encourage more innovation like this, either virtual programs or otherwise, with the goal of increasing availability to job seekers, particularly in rural areas?

Answer 3. To assist me in answering this question, I have consulted with Ronald Painter, the Chief Executive Officer of the National Association of Workforce Boards, who is available for any followup questions in this area. Job postings are generally handled almost entirely on-line, so for that function many job seekers are able to find what they need without ever coming to a center.

In addition to virtual centers, many areas also turn to their local libraries, which are far more numerous than One-Stop centers, for help in administering some of the One-Stop functions. Mobile offices are also used in these areas.

While the use of virtual centers may provide some workers with easier access to services, there are some caveats. Surveys have suggested, for instance, that many people use a physical center because they feel more connected and comfortable "talking" to someone about their situations and options. So, virtual offices would need to have a good counseling system available. The Canadians have developed some good models of both eCounseling and eMentoring, so it is possible. On a similar note, proper assessment of the worker's needs can sometimes be difficult in a virtual setting, especially a full assessment of the worker's "soft skills."

QUESTIONS OF SENATOR BENNET

Question 1. What role can business play in furthering workforce development? Are there on-the-ground examples of private sector initiatives that have helped to close skill gaps in our economy? Where do you think the law can be improved to foster more partnerships between business and workforce development providers? What are some ways that the private sector, government, non-profits and labor can partner in the development of our workforce?

Answer 1. There are numerous examples of private sector initiatives aimed at closing skills gaps in the economy. One such example is the Walmart Workforce and Economic Opportunity Initiative, a 2-year $2.5 million initiative sponsored by the Walmart Foundation. The initiative is administered by the AACCs' Center for Workforce and Economic Development in collaboration with the National Center on Education and the Economy. The purpose is to develop regional approaches to adult and post-secondary education, workforce, and economic development. Twenty community colleges will receive $100,000 in funding and technical assistance for 2 years. The aims of this program are to:

• Improve leadership capacity of rural and remote college partnerships in response to regional labor-market needs.

• Increase the number of community colleges coordinating education, workforce, and economic development to support regional growth.

• Strengthen accountability.

• Raise recognition of, and support for, education and workforce development as economic development tools.

In reauthorizing WIA, we must make changes to the law to make the system more relevant to our business partners. Despite the fact that the law now mandates business leadership and majorities on the workforce investment boards, in some places the business community seems to feel that the boards are often too large, too bogged down in operational details, and not engaged in the high-level strategic planning that is the best use of the business partners' time. For this reason, Congress should re-examine what is in the law regarding the makeup of the boards and the language describing their missions and make any changes necessary to bring about the vision of the boards that was originally intended.

WIA should also encourage more innovative structures for the delivery of services to workers and businesses alike. Sector-based strategies are one way to effectively keep the focus on what is needed by both of these constituencies in a structured and efficient way. These strategies should involve all the key stakeholders, including those cited in your question. The key advantage of approaching an area's workforce needs through the prism of a sector strategy, if done effectively, is that the system will better maintain the interest of the involved business community, as opposed to a more generalized workforce development strategy.

Question 2. Do you find the current workforce development system to be responsive to emerging industries and employment opportunities in energy and health care? Do you find the training in these fields and resources required for such training to be different? Are there training models on the State level that we should replicate nationally?

Answer 2. The current workforce development system, with its Federal funding and regulatory mandates layered with additional State funding and policy oversight, does not appear to respond quickly to emerging industries and employment opportunities in energy and health care. The clear focus of the current workforce development system is to align job seekers and businesses as efficiently as possible, in order to quickly train and transition unemployed workers into employment. Federal program performance measures, especially through the Workforce Investment Act (WIA), focus exclusively on job placement rates, compensation rates and retention, regardless of an existing or emerging industry.

We know that the energy and health care industries are experiencing tremendous workforce challenges, as technology improves, demands continue to increase and the marketplace continues to evolve. The training requirements for both of these industries are a particular challenge as the workforce requirements are rapidly being updated, yet many education and training organizations are not able to stay current with updated marketplace demands. Funding constraints, especially on public-funded training institutions, limit our ability to lead students into emerging industry occupations without substantial funding support and leadership from private sector businesses who simply cannot wait for newly trained workers to materialize.

_____

ATTACHMENT A—AACC WIA REAUTHORIZATION PRIORITIES

In reauthorizing the Workforce Investment Act (WIA), Congress should reform the workforce system with the goal of providing workers access to the post-secondary education and training they need to support families in today's economy. In turn, businesses will be provided with the skilled workers they need to prosper. Currently, WIA and other workforce development programs are not doing enough to establish clear and multiple pathways to post-secondary education and training for workers, especially those with low-skill levels. To do this, the workforce investment system must spur greater degrees of innovation and collaboration between key stakeholders at all levels.

Community colleges have had varied experiences under WIA. Some of them have played integral roles in the system by being active members of State and local workforce investment boards, hosting and running One-Stop Career Centers, and training great numbers of WIA participants. Other colleges, conversely, have played little or no role in the system, as addressed below. Too often, community colleges are mere vendors in a system in which they should be true partners.

A successful workforce system cannot afford to underutilize community colleges in this way. Whether it be educating low-skilled adults and those with limited English proficiency and transitioning them to post-secondary education, developing and offering cutting edge occupational programs, working directly with businesses to help train their workers, or running programs that combine all three of these aspects and more, community colleges are a natural hub of the workforce development system.

AACC urges Congress to give community colleges a central role in the WIA system. With the expected passage of the American Graduation Initiative early next year, the Administration and Congress will invest substantial resources in community colleges to help the Nation raise its level of higher education attainment. WIA reauthorization should be viewed as the next phase in serving that broader goal.

Some States have already featured community colleges in their workforce development initiatives. On a national level, however, WIA is essentially agnostic as to training providers. Prioritizing the role of community colleges is key to strengthening the system overall. Community colleges are the closest thing this country has to a national network of ubiquitous, low-cost and high-quality training providers, and the WIA legislation should reflect that.

Community colleges join other stakeholders in the workforce system in supporting new directions and innovations in the provision of services to WIA participants, including sector initiatives, regional partnerships, and above all greater alignment between programs, particularly WIA titles I and II.

With this guiding principle in mind, the following are top issues for community colleges in WIA reauthorization.

INCREASE THE QUANTITY AND QUALITY OF TRAINING UNDER WIA

1. Provide More Support for the Expansion of Training Capacity: Community colleges place top priority on efforts to help students access post-secondary education and training. However, many community colleges are straining to serve all the students who are enrolling. In economic downturns such as the one we are now experiencing, double-digit percentage increases in enrollment from 1 year to the next are the norm. These enrollment increases are often not covered by State appropriations, so colleges are forced to raise tuition (if they have that authority), cut expenses to the bone, or turn students away from their programs. Often, it will be a combination of all three. The average community college derives approximately 20 percent of its revenue through tuition and fees, which gives some idea of the percentage of the college's actual program costs that are covered by individual training accounts.

Simply put, community colleges do not need to recruit to draw additional students, but those students place a great burden on the community college education and training services. Our member institutions further believe that they should be the primary provider of training services in the workforce development system. For this reason, AACC urges Congress to emphasize direct support for additional training capacity at community colleges in a reauthorized WIA. Without a Federal priority on developing this capacity, WIA participants will continue to face less effective, more expensive options if they wish to immediately access training. Businesses will struggle to find candidates with the skills that they need for available jobs.

Congress can take some simple, but meaningful, steps in this direction under the current WIA structure:

• First, it should authorize the Community-Based Job Training Grants (CBJTGs), which were created in 2004 in response to this capacity crunch. The CBJTGs are a sector initiative that is funded and is working. The program should be authorized as it was originally envisioned, namely a national competitive grant program that awards grants to community colleges, working in partnership with local WIBs, businesses and other key stakeholders to expand training capacity at the college and train workers for high-demand occupations.

• Second, it should give local boards greater flexibility to utilize training contracts, especially with low-tuition training providers such as community colleges. This approach was taken in the American Recovery and Reinvestment Act because Congress recognized it as a way to expeditiously and effectively train workers and stimulate the economy. It should be made a permanent part of WIA.

2. Encourage Innovative Modes of Delivering Training and Other Services: AACC also urges Congress to think more broadly about the most effective ways to deliver WIA funds at the regional and local level, to ensure the proper mix between assisting participant access to training and the development of training capacity.

• **Authorize Sector Initiatives:** Sector initiatives bring together training providers, businesses, WIBs, economic development and other key partners to develop training programs and train workers and provide other services to help important local business sectors thrive. These initiatives are a particularly effective way of ensuring that workers are receiving training for available, good jobs. WIA should provide State and local areas with ample space to design such initiatives that best suit their needs. However, community colleges should be key partners in any such program that receives WIA support. The CBJTG program provides a model that should be used when designing sector initiatives within the WIA formula programs.

• **Establish Incentive Grants to Reward Innovative and Effective Programs:** Incentive grants should reward more than just meeting a numerical benchmark, but instead they should spur the innovative, effective and coordinated approaches devised at the State and local levels that other areas should emulate. Effective utilization of community colleges should be one factor in deciding the grant recipients.

3. Remove Current Impediments to Quality Training

• **Eliminate the Sequence of Services:** Many local areas proceed under the assumption that WIA participants must go through core and intensive services before they are able to access training. WIA should explicitly state that, when an initial screening shows that they would benefit from it, WIA participants are able to immediately access training.

• **Modify the Performance Indicators to Recognize Skill Attainment and Allow for Longer Term Training:** The WIA performance indicators have a tremendous impact on the attitude of local boards and One-Stop Career Centers to the longer term training that many workers need, especially low-skilled workers. The current performance indicators, which put a heavy emphasis on job placement, retention and earning, are "work first" measures. They should be modified to count interim and progressive indicators of skill attainment, including measures of "work readiness" for very low-skilled workers.

• **Streamline Trainer Eligibility:** Quality control of training providers should be retained. There remain many training providers of suspect quality who would like to participate in the system in hopes of attracting WIA participants and the training funds that come with them. However, eligibility requirements should not drive quality trainers away from the system. Numerous community colleges cite the current eligibility requirements as a reason for their limited or non-participation in the WIA system, especially the requirement to track non-WIA participants in any program they seek to make eligible.

AACC supports the direction that legislation in previous Congresses took in regard to the trainer eligibility provisions, but believes that new legislation should take one more step. Public institutions of higher education should be deemed automatically eligible as training providers. These institutions are subject to accreditation, State performance requirements, and other Federal reporting requirements that are more than enough to ensure they meet a quality threshold for participation in the workforce system. They are not the providers of questionable quality and motives that eligibility requirements should seek to weed out.

Automatic eligibility for public institutions of higher education is not a "free pass" for these providers, nor will it result in a loss of crucial information. The success of these training providers in serving WIA participants would still be tracked through the WIA performance measures, and this information would still be available to WIA participants who are choosing among training providers. However, the current statute seems to have blurred the issues of basic eligibility and performance measurement with its extensive and burdensome eligibility requirements.

STRENGTHEN PATHWAYS TO POST-SECONDARY EDUCATION AND TRAINING

1. Adult Basic Education: The Nation's economy requires that an unprecedented number and percentage of the population enter and succeed in post-secondary education and training. Achieving these goals will require a multi-faceted effort on the parts of institutions, States and the Federal Government. This effort will only succeed if we are effective in reaching out to populations that are currently underrepresented in post-secondary education. In WIA reauthorization, Congress has a significant opportunity to assist this effort by providing support for increased linkages between adult basic education, workforce training and post-secondary education. The ABE to post-secondary "pipeline" is vital to achieving the post-secondary participation rates that will be necessary to maintaining this Nation's quality of life. The recent increase in the number of States where the community college system administers the adult education program reflects this. To improve the functioning of the ABE to post-secondary pipeline, we recommend the following:

• Add "transition to post-secondary education and training" to the purposes of the act and the definition of adult education, and clarify throughout the act that transition programs can and should be funded with adult education funds.

• Require consultation between the eligible State agency under the Adult Education Act and other key WIA stakeholders, including the State community college system, both in the development of the State plan and in the awarding of grants or contracts to eligible providers.

• Include a measure of the total number of people served by the adult education system who make the transition to post-secondary education and training in the performance accountability system.

• Require eligible agencies to consider, when deciding on local grants and contracts, whether grantees offer post-secondary transition programs, with special consideration given to programs that are administered by an institution of higher education or take place on the campus of an institution of higher education.

• In addition, AACC urges Congress to create a new national program that would nurture and disseminate innovative approaches bridging the current gap between adult basic education and post-secondary education and training. Community colleges believe that there is a vital Federal role to play in spurring greater activity in this area. The Federal Government played a similar role in driving the development of high school/college dual enrollment programs, now a vital pathway to college for millions of students, through the former Tech Prep Demonstration program. We envision a similar approach here.

• Finally, Congress should not view adult basic education only through the lens of title II. The need for these services is so vast that we must find ways to better integrate basic skills (including English language) and occupational training within the title I programs. Career pathways are an essential strategy to achieving these ends. Many of the recommendations above, especially modifying the performance indicators to allow for longer term training and awarding innovative training programs, would help with this.

2. Youth Services: For the same reasons that apply to adult basic education, Congress must also prioritize youth programs that have strong connections to post-secondary education. Indeed, there is tremendous overlap in the populations served by the youth services and adult basic education programs when the youth age is extended to 24. Yet, despite what they have to offer, community colleges are even perhaps less involved in the youth programs than any other aspect of WIA. AACC urges Congress to apply its recommendations for bolstering the connection between adult basic education and post-secondary education to the youth programs as well.

IMPROVE WIA GOVERNANCE AND OPERATIONS

1. **Streamline Workforce Boards:** Congress should redouble its efforts to bring together key stakeholders in States, regions and localities to plan efficient and effective workforce and economic development activities. These partnerships should always include community college representation. The concept and the implementation of workforce boards must be flexible enough to adapt to any workforce development strategies that may play a greater role in a reauthorized WIA, such as the regional and sectoral initiatives that have shown tremendous promise. The authorizers must also carefully consider the stakeholders that truly need to be at the table when determining the minimum required board memberships. The partnerships that run successful regional and sectoral partnerships, including those under the WIRED initiative and the Community-Based Job Training Grants, should serve as models for modified board composition.

Community college leaders report frustration with large boards that become mired in operational details rather than focusing on leadership at a higher level, as was originally intended. AACC believes that businesses should retain a strong role in these partnerships, but some colleges report that the business-majority requirement can create situations where business owners that are not truly qualified to help lead the community's workforce and economic development efforts are included on boards, simply to come up with the required number of businesses. This is especially the case in rural areas. Board membership should be strictly limited to high-level leaders at the respective institutions to ensure the proper focus on the big picture.

2. **Directly Support Infrastructure:** The current system, which calls on partners to come together at the local level to contribute to the costs of running One-Stop centers, has not worked satisfactorily in many areas. However, proposals to divert funds from these partner programs at the State level are also unsatisfactory, particularly since most of the partner programs have suffered their own funding cuts in recent years. AACC urges Congress to authorize a line-item authorization for directly supporting the infrastructure of the Federal workforce development system.

The goal of avoiding duplication of effort and inefficiency is laudatory, but not achieved through the forced marriage of partner programs. Post-Secondary Perkins Act and adult basic education funds support program improvement, not core and other services, so there is no redundancy between these programs and One-Stop services that is prevented by diverting funds from these programs into the One-Stop infrastructure. Instead, all a diversion of funds from these partner programs achieves is a diminution of their effectiveness.

AACC is mindful of the potential pitfall that comes with a line item for infrastructure: that funding for this item would come at the expense of other WIA funding. However, if Congress believes the Federal workforce development system to be a worthy endeavor, and community colleges believe it is, then it should support it directly.

3. **Encourage Alignment of WIA and Community College Service Areas:** One characteristic that many States and areas which enjoy high levels of community college integration into the workforce system is the alignment of community college and WIA local service areas. In many such instances, community colleges also house the One-Stop Career Centers, bringing a greater degree of coordination between the two systems. WIA should encourage States to adopt such alignments.

ADDITIONAL RECOMMENDATIONS

1. **Increase Support for Entrepreneurship Programs:** Heretofore primarily seen as an economic development activity, development and support of entrepreneurs must be a heightened priority in WIA. Community colleges offer certificate and degree programs for entrepreneurs and many directly support fledgling enterprises through business incubator initiatives. These activities are especially important in rural areas. A reauthorized WIA should allow training dollars to be used for entrepreneurial programs; remove any obstacles to using WIA resources, in tan-

dem with economic development and other resources, to support entrepreneurial incubators and similar initiatives; and increase coordination with the Small Business Administration and other sources of Federal support for entrepreneurs.

2. **Effectively Utilize Labor Exchange Information:** Timely and accurate information about available jobs and other labor market conditions is an essential tool for job seekers and workforce development providers alike. WIA should creatively integrate the effective use of services such as the public-private Jobs Central to more efficiently and effectively match applicants with jobs and help providers understand local labor markets better so they can design relevant training opportunities that lead to real jobs. Effective use of these systems would help move unemployment insurance recipients into jobs more quickly and help to identify those in need of more services.

[Whereupon, at 12:41 p.m., the hearing was adjourned.]

○